Social Studies:

Applications for a New Century

Social Studies:

Applications for a New Century

Sarah S. Pate
The University of Alabama

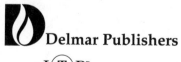

Delmar Publishers

I(T)P™

Albany • Bonn • Boston • Cincinnati • Detroit • London • Madrid • Melbourne
Mexico City • New York • Pacific Grove • Paris • San Francisco • Singapore • Tokyo
Toronto • Washington

NOTICE TO THE READER

Publisher does not warrant or guarantee any of the products described herein or perform any independent analysis in connection with any of the product information contained herein. Publisher does not assume, and expressly disclaims, any obligation to obtain and include information other than that provided to it by the manufacturer.

The reader is expressly warned to consider and adopt all safety precautions that might be indicated by the activities herein and to avoid all potential hazards. By following the instructions contained herein, the reader willingly assumes all risks in connection with such instructions.

The publisher makes no representations or warranties of any kind, including but not limited to, the warranties of fitness for particular purpose or merchantability, nor are any such representations implied with respect to the material set forth herein, and the publisher takes no responsibility with respect to such material. The publisher shall not be liable for any special, consequential, or exemplary damages resulting, in whole or in part, from the readers' use of, or reliance upon, this material.

Cover Design: Spiral Design

Delmar staff:
Publisher: Diane McOscar
Associate Editor: Erin J. O'Connor
Production Coordinator: Sandra Woods
Art and Design Coordinator: Timothy J. Conners

COPYRIGHT © 1996
by Delmar Publishers Inc.
a division of International Thomson Publishing Inc.

I(T)P   The ITP logo is a trademark under license.

Printed in the United States of America

For more information, contact:
Delmar Publishers
3 Columbia Circle, Box 15015
Albany, New York 12212-5015

International Thomson Publishing
Berkshire House
168-173 High Holborn
London, WC1V 7AA
England

Thomas Nelson Australia
102 Dodds Street
South Melbourne 3205
Victoria, Australia

Nelson Canada
1120 Birchmont Road
Scarborough, Ontario
M1K 5G4, Canada

International Thomson Editores
Campos Eliseos 385, Piso 7
Col Polonco
11660 Mexico D F Mexico

International Thomson Publishing GmbH
Konigswinterer Str. 418
53227 Bonn
Germany

International Thomson Publishing Asia
221 Henderson Bldg. #05-10
Singapore 0315

International Thomson Publishing Japan
Kyowa Building, 3F
2-2-1 Hirakawa-cho
Chiyoda-ku, Tokyo 102
Japan

1 2 3 4 5 6 7 8 9 10 XXX 01 00 99 98 97 96 95

Library of Congress Cataloging-in-Publication Data

Pate, Sarah S.
      Social studies : applications for a new century / Sarah S. Pate.
          p.   cm.
      Includes bibliographical references and index.
      ISBN 0-8273-6637-X
      1. Social sciences—Study and teaching—United States.   I. Title.
LB1584.P285   1995
372.83'044—dc20
                              95-34828
                              CIP

Contents

Preface

The purpose of the text is to provide a resource of information, ideas, and activities that current and future classroom teachers might use in helping students become more familiar with concepts and skills needed to be successful in developing a working knowledge in the content area of social studies. The book is designed for use by educators working primarily with students at the elementary and middle school levels; however, some information is applicable for lower elementary levels.

In each unit, explanation is given concerning the rationale or usefulness of the material included in the unit. For the benefit of those persons enrolled in education courses, each unit has an introduction to provide information from a content or theoretical base.

Also in each unit, examples, charts, graphs, and/or appropriate photographs are included to provide further explanation of information.

The book is primarily divided into three sections. The first section provides general information for the teacher about the area of social studies. The middle section of the book provides a number of activity ideas and the rationale for their use. The final section of the book is a summary of the information presented as well as suggestions for possible future directions for social studies.

This differs from a number of other texts and resource books in design, that is, both general information and activity ideas are presented. In addition, general information is stressed; no specific ideas or models are deemed the one best method, which is often a problem in texts.

As mentioned previously, examples, activities, and graphic aids are consistently provided throughout this book. Actual lesson plans that have been implemented in normal elementary classrooms are used as examples. Case studies or examples of actual events in classrooms related to the area of social studies instruction are provided throughout the informational portion of this book.

Study questions are provided at the beginning of each section to guide the reader. At the end of each section, helpful hints for implementation of the information are provided.

The book is designed for use by current classroom practitioners or students planning to teach at the elementary or middle school levels. The book is written as a basic informational source and as an activity and resource book.

As a prerequisite for using this book, it is important that readers have a basic knowledge of characteristics of learners at various levels. It also is important that readers be familiar with basic educational jargon so as to develop a clear understanding of the intent of the information presented.

To Bobby, who has given me support, encouragement,
and understanding patience throughout
each step of the way in this and all
professional endeavors.

To my family, colleagues, and past
and present students, who
have been instrumental
in providing
encouragement.

About This Resource

Why another social studies book? Why do I, an educator, need to look at, much less read this book? Is it worth my time (and money)?

Being a certified professional educator for a number of years, and being a member of the same group as current and future classroom practitioners, I can truthfully understand the logic and/or reason behind each of these questions. In order to find an answer to these questions, it is my hope that you will take the time to look through the book and decide for yourself.

As an undergraduate student, classroom practitioner, and professor at the post-secondary level, my experiences with education-related books has led me to believe that they basically fall into two categories: text format or resource/activity format. This book is different in that it is a resource/activity book and a textbook combined. The purpose behind the book is to provide a resource of information, ideas, and activities that current and future classroom practitioners might use in helping students become more familiar with concepts and skills needed to be successful in the content area of social studies. The book is designed for use by educators who currently are or are planning to work with students at the elementary (grades 1–6) and middle school (grades 5–8) levels.

Information in the book moves from basic information about the area of social studies and instruction to activities that may be used as a part of lessons. For the benefit of those persons enrolled in education courses, each section will have an introduction to provide information from a content or theoretical base. The book provides a rationale for each of the activity examples provided.

Outstanding features of the book which make it especially useful or usable include:

1. Readability: Unlike some texts which go on forever before they get to the point, information is presented in clear, concise, readable terms. Jargon used is easily understood by persons with a basic background in the area of education. Current classroom practitioners as well as future teachers are not talked down to by the language used.

2. Number of graphic aids: The old adage "a picture is worth a thousand words" describes an outstanding feature of the book. We, as educators, expect our elementary and middle school students to make use of the graphic aids in textbooks, yet those books we use in college education courses or teachers' resource centers often leave us to develop our own ideas and perceptions of descriptions. The

proposed book will include an abundance of appropriate examples which may be used as a springboard for instructional ideas.

3. Activities: Instead of being a textbook made up of a great deal of narrative with only a limited number of activity suggestions, the book provides a number of ideas and activities which may be used by the reader, whether currently a classroom practitioner or an education student in a field experience setting.

4. Sources of information: In planning this book, I based the focus on those areas of need and interest mentioned by current classroom practitioners and education students over a number of years. In addition, I looked back at my own classroom experiences and those of the students I have had the opportunity to work with. Finally, but importantly, the information disseminated by professional organizations such as The National Council for the Social Studies, International Reading Association, National Council of Teachers of English, Middle School Association, and Association for Childhood International as well as a number of other professional organizations, provide the basis for information included in the book.

STUDY QUESTIONS FOR UNIT 1: **1.** How does one define the term social studies? **2.** What other areas of education may have an influence on what is taught in social studies? **3.** What are three theories about how social studies education should be developed? **4.** What is meant by Teacher-Guided Lessons? Expository? Demonstration? Semantic Mapping? Directed Learning Activity (DLA)? **5.** What is meant by Learner Involvement Lessons? Activity lessons? Cooperative Learning? Simulation? Individualized instruction? **6.** Why are resources other than textbooks and encyclopedias important in social studies

For the Student/Teacher

education? **7.** Describe two uses of bulletin boards in social studies education **8.** How may current affairs be most effectively used in social studies education?

INTRODUCTION The purpose of this unit is to provide the teacher with some general information pertaining to the area of instruction or, more specifically, to the area of instruction as it relates to social studies. In order to accomplish the goal of a general overview of social studies instruction there are a number of specifics which will be discussed, including a history of social studies, a definition of social studies, information about and suggestions for use of teacher-guided lessons and learner involvement lessons, suggestions for use of resources in social studies instruction, and a reacquaintance with the use of bulletin boards and current affairs in social studies.

WHAT ARE THE SOCIAL STUDIES?

Upon hearing the term social studies, what comes to mind? Do you remember dressing up like "Indians" around Thanksgiving? Or do you possibly relate the term to the memorization of the names and capitals of the 50 United States? Another memory of social studies which some people have is of visiting the state capital or some other place of historical significance. Basically, for a number of people whether they be in the field of education or another profession, social studies as a memorable past school experience is not a reality. There are numerous individual reasons this is the case, but for the sake of argument, only two will be mentioned. The first reason is that social studies as a subject has not been at the forefront of the focus of education, whereas reading, math, and science (off and on) have received more emphasis up until the last ten to fifteen years depending on locality in our country. A second reason that social studies has been somewhat neglected is, similar to science, simply the fact that a great number of teachers have not felt adequately prepared in the area and therefore have limited their teaching strategies for social studies to the textbook (i.e., read, lecture, answer questions) or those activities which their grandmother's teacher used (i.e., dressing up, celebrating holidays, or drawing maps).

Up until the early 1900s, there was little consensus regarding the curriculum topics for instruction within the area. Much like the social studies experiences some of us remember from our past, social studies instruction was described as great festivals (referring to holiday celebrations) (Wade, 1911, p. 25), study of the cave man, and Indians (Steel, 1911, p. 45).

Some school districts did not include any instruction in the content areas now considered a part of social studies until third grade or higher (Croswell, 1897). Other districts introduced instruction in history and geography at various grade levels; however, there was no one definition of what was to be included in social studies nor was there any consensus on the order for introduction (Croswell, 1897).

Given the growth in the areas of psychology, sociology, and anthropology following the turn of the century, more attention was focused on the development of social studies as a combination of content areas. In addition, a plan for a curriculum that recognized the stages of child development as an important component of instruction led to the definition of social studies as a subject area (Hall, 1901).

Social studies as a combined content area was defined by the National Education Association (NEA) in the early 1900s (Barnard, 1913; Jones et al., 1926). The definition of social studies has undergone a number of changes over time to reflect the ever increasing understanding of how children develop, the influences of society, and the influences of technological advancements on our society.

Given this background, the first matter which needs to be undertaken is the definition of social studies. According to the National Council for the Social Studies, the social studies may be defined as

> . . . a basic subject of the K–12 curriculum that derives its goals from the nature of citizenship in a democratic society that is closely linked to other nations and peoples of the world; draws its content primarily from history, the social sciences, and in some respects, from the humanities and science; is taught in ways that reflect an awareness of the personal, social, and cultural experiences and developmental levels of learners; and facilitates the transfer of what is learned in school to the out-of-school lives of students. (NCSS, 1990)

While this definition is quite understandable, a working definition that we, as teachers, can identify with seems more appropriate. Social studies may be broadly defined as the study of the past, present, and prospects for the future; the study of the social and life skills needed to become productive citizens in a changing world, and the knowledge of the surroundings (local and worldwide) needed by all global citizens. Social studies is a complex content area as well as a very subjective content area. Because of these two factors, it is often neglected or rushed through. According to several school-based practitioners who gladly shared their perspective on social studies, it is a content area that is important in theory but at times presents frustration because of its subjectiveness and constant mode of change.

Social studies is not a single area of thought. It includes information from a number of other areas, such as history, anthropology, archeology, geography, science, and the arts and humanities. In order to be successful in teaching social studies, it is important that a teacher come to grips with the fact that there are no exact boundaries for social studies; that is, a number of traditional areas are included in social studies, so by form it is an integrated curriculum. In addition, teachers need to understand that the area of social studies is systematic and sequential, that is, students

FIGURE 1-1 Spiraling Curriculum

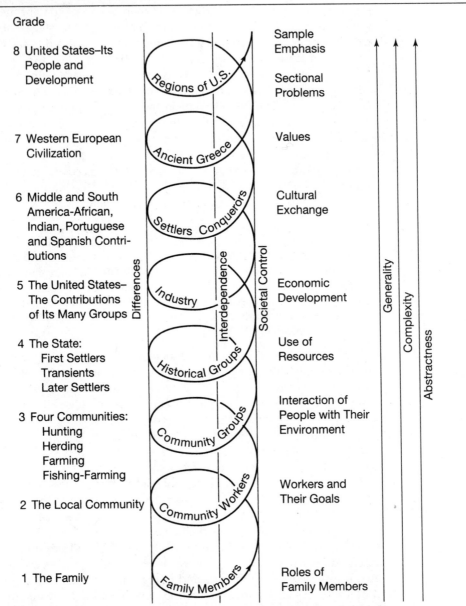

SOURCE: "The Spiral Development of Three Key Concepts" (Fig. 1) from *Teacher's Handbook for Elementary Social Studies,* 2nd ed., by Hilda Taba, Copyright © 1971. Addison-Wesley Publishing Company. Reprinted with permission.

TABLE 1-1 The Expanding Environments Approach to Social Studies

KINDERGARTEN	**THIRD GRADE**	**SIXTH GRADE**
Self	Communities	World cultures
School		Western hemisphere studies
Community	**FOURTH GRADE**	
Home	State history	**SEVENTH GRADE**
	Geographic regions	World geography or history
FIRST GRADE		
Families	**FIFTH GRADE**	**EIGHTH GRADE**
	History of the United States	American history
SECOND GRADE		
Neighborhoods		

---

need to develop social studies knowledge (including skills) in a certain order for maximum understanding (Jarolimek, 1993). Social studies is two-sided in that it includes processes and products. The process part of social studies is the search for patterns or information. The product part is the end result or the facts, concepts, and generalizations being searched for (Sunal, 1990).

Given this information, a number of theories about how students should be guided in their social studies education have developed. One of these is the *Spiraling Curriculum,* proposed by Hilda Taba (1971). (See Figure 1-1.) The basic focus of this suggested curriculum is the development of knowledge by repeating information on a higher or more abstract level as the students progress through the educational system. While there are merits to this system, it is important in implementing a curriculum based on this model that students are actually receiving instruction on higher or more abstract levels and not just repeating the same information. The curriculum seemingly used most often is the *Expanding Environments Approach,* in which the students expand out from their own environment to study a worldwide view (Superka, Hawke, & Morrissett, 1980).

While the expanding environments approach has been the basis for the traditional social studies curriculum for a number of years (Superka et al., 1980; Morrissett, 1981; Baskerville & Sesow, 1976), there has been criticism of the approach. The view that students come to school with knowledge of their family and community has come under fire. Critics maintain that students in today's world are exposed to issues and events that take place far from their local environment prior to entering school (Naylor & Diem, 1977; Chapin & Messick, 1992). Another criticism of the approach is that it does not address issues of current importance to

FIGURE 1-2 General Social Studies Curriculum: Umbrella Approach

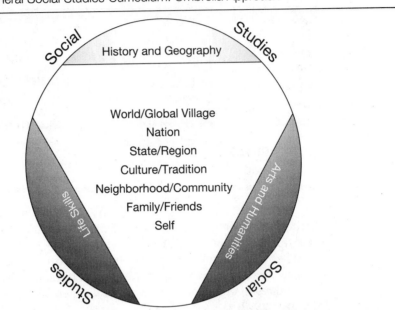

students (i.e., an issue outside the pattern of study) (Joyce & Alleman-Brooks, 1982). While the criticism may be well-founded, partial responsibility for the modification of any curriculum to meet specific student needs must be accepted by the teacher.

Rather than try to develop a totally new suggestion for curriculum, the goal should be to try to take those that are available, and build one that will work for a particular school community. Special emphasis should be given to skills areas, yet, at the same time, it is equally important for teachers to understand how social studies should be a grounding point for human relations skills development. With this in mind, the following basic suggestion is made for a general social studies curriculum for students in grade levels K–8. (See Figure 1-2.)

CURRICULUM FOR SOCIAL STUDIES: UMBRELLA APPROACH

When viewing the total curriculum traditionally followed at the elementary and middle school levels, there are distinct divisions between the content areas. Math, science, English and language arts, and social studies are usually found as core subjects with art, music, and physical education being included as well. While it is important for educators to recognize the students' need for knowledge within each distinct area, it is also important that students learn the relationship between the areas as well. An umbrella curriculum that purposefully provides students with this information is highly recommended as a possible curriculum.

In understanding an umbrella curriculum, we must first come to an agreement on a definition of the term. An umbrella curriculum may be defined as an interdisciplinary curriculum:

> A knowledge view and curriculum approach that purposefully draws knowledge, perspectives, and methods of inquiry from more than one discipline together to examine a central theme, problem, person or event (Jacobs, 1989).

Social studies by definition is an integrated content area. Its foundation includes information from a number of distinct traditional areas including history, geography, sociology, anthropology, economics, political science, and psychology. In addition, the arts and humanities are important aspects of the social studies, especially as related to cultural studies. Finally, life skills needed by students as they develop into productive citizens now and in the future round out the information covered in social studies.

Because of the broad foundation of social studies as a content area, it is an ideal area to serve as an umbrella in viewing the total curriculum. It is important that we understand that while an umbrella curriculum is needed to help students develop an understanding on given topics, study of the distinct disciplines is important and should not be totally abandoned. Basic skills particular to each area should still be focused on as needed for building students' background knowledge.

An umbrella curriculum should be used as a tool to help students expand and refine their knowledge. It should seek to integrate different components or aspects of a particular topic so that students will see the topic more clearly. For example, study of the westward movement could be combined with a look at American literature of that time. While students are learning information about the experiences encountered by those who were a part of the movement, they are also learning specific facts related to the movement (e.g., transportation, number of miles covered per day, why certain towns were established).

Other examples for integrating traditional content areas under the umbrella of social studies include the formation of actual companies such as "The Tomato Factory," where third graders engage in experiences such as developing labels for their canned products, marketing strategies, and recipes that use their product. This activity would encompass traditional areas of language arts, economics, math, and art. Another example would be an integration of science, math, language arts, and geography by planting flowers or tree seedlings at various places around the school and having students keep records of growth.

While looking at the positive aspects that an umbrella curriculum can have, it is equally important to be aware of the negative outcomes that are possible. First and foremost, educators need to select the topics and methods for completing a study carefully so as to maintain the importance of each discipline represented. In doing this, the educator must make the students aware of the various content areas being explored rather than minimizing the importance of the skills they should be expanding and refining.

Another negative outcome involves choosing only one method for instruction. As stated before, while an umbrella curriculum is ideal for a vast number of topics, skills, and concepts, there are times when presentation in the distinct areas would be more beneficial for the development of long-term understanding or use by the students. For example, looking at the maps used by certain explorers as they crossed Mexico may be interesting, but only after students have developed basic map reading skills or are able to understand the legends used in describing the various graphic information about the land. In addition, basic math skills which would be needed in order for students to measure distances accurately would probably be better taught with a focus on mathematic principles.

Finally, educators need to view the curriculum they are attempting to implement as a whole, not as bits and pieces or a quick and easy method for improvement in instruction. We have a tendency, in education, to jump on the proverbial bandwagon of any new buzzword. Educators are often guilty of modifying the curriculum based on a new buzzword despite what they know about how students learn or they make no modifications at all but use the same instructional strategies for all classes. The topics one might use with group A in a study following an umbrella approach may be inappropriate for group B. And what worked last year should not necessarily be used again this year.

In summary, use of good professional judgement on how and when students should engage in certain strategies for learning information must be made by the educator involved with them on a daily basis. While social studies is an ideal area for the foundation of an umbrella curriculum, it is by no means an end in itself when helping students develop necessary life skills in order to be productive citizens now and in the future.

Keeping in mind all of the information discussed so far, the question that needs to be addressed is "How does one go about teaching in the area of social studies?" While there are many techniques for instruction, and many facets of each technique, the goal is to provide students with information in ways that allow them to develop an understanding of the material in relation to their everyday lives, in and out of the school setting. Two main techniques or strategies for instruction include *Teacher-Guided Lessons* and *Learner Involvement Lessons.*

TEACHER-GUIDED LESSONS

Usually when we hear the term teacher-guided lesson, we think of formal strategies of instruction with special emphasis on expository strategies. In actuality, *teacher-guided lessons* can be used to describe a number of less

---

FIGURE 1-3 Example of an Expository Lesson

Teacher: Ms. Lockett   **Subject:** Social Studies

Grade: 3rd   **Lesson Topic:** Thanksgiving

Grouping Strategy (Predominant): Whole Group

Objectives: The students will demonstrate an understanding of how the Native Americans helped the Pilgrims when they first arrived in the New World.

INSTRUCTIONAL PROCEDURES:	MATERIALS:
1. Have the students come to a circle on the story rug.	Story rug
2. Motivate students by asking questions about information related to Thanksgiving.	
Examples: What do you know about Thanksgiving?	
What do we usually eat on Thanksgiving?	
Why do we celebrate Thanksgiving?	
3. Read *Thanksgiving Day* by Gail Gibbons.	Book: *Thanksgiving Day* by G. Gibbons
4. After reading the story, talk about why the Pilgrims left their home to find a new land.	
5. Explain to the students ways the Native Americans helped the Pilgrims to adjust to the new land.	
6. After telling how the Native Americans helped the Pilgrims adjust, discuss why Native Americans used pictographs to write.	Chart of symbols
7. Provide time for the students to ask questions.	

EVALUATION:

    STUDENT: The students will be evaluated through their participation.

    TEACHER: Were materials used sufficient to explain the information to the students?
                   Did the students actively participate?

formal strategies which may be implemented to help students attain knowledge. Some of these strategies include use of demonstration lessons, semantic mapping, and variations of the directed learning activity.

Expository strategies of instruction are those that beginning teachers may feel most comfortable in using; this was one of the most prevalent strategies until experience was gained. There are situations when even experienced teachers may implement expository teaching; however, this is not a commonly used strategy for everyday instruction by experienced teachers. In expository strategies there are a number of components the teacher controls carefully. The teacher: (1) preselects the information to be studied, (2) decides on the objectives to be achieved, (3) selects the types and amount of material to be used during instruction, and (4) sets the timeline for covering the information. In addition, expository teaching strategies are somewhat teacher oriented, leaving little time for student interaction or for independent work by students.

Management is generally not a problem for the teacher using an expository method of instruction because of the focus on the teacher and material. However, caution must be taken by a teacher implementing the expository strategy so that the various learning needs of the students are being met. The structure of the expository lesson may be frustrating to students who are not reading on the same level as the material, who have no interest in the topic of study, or who have a great deal of background knowledge about the topic of study but cannot share it due to the limited amount of student input usually allowed in an expository lesson.

This same caution must be taken when using demonstration lessons. Demonstration lessons may be included as a component in other strategies or may be used as a single, basic strategy for instruction. Much like the expository strategy, the teacher has a great amount of control. She preselects the information to be studied, the materials to be used, the objectives, and the time frame for the demonstration. In demonstration lessons, the teacher is actively involved in the presentation of information by telling, showing, or doing.

It is important for the teacher to consider carefully the makeup of the class when planning a demonstration lesson. The information to be studied and the materials to be used need to be such that the students will maintain interest. It is also imperative that the teacher keep in mind the ability levels, maturity levels, and background experiences of the students for whom the demonstration lesson will be made.

A key component of demonstration lessons is the interaction which takes place as a part of the lesson. While there is some student interaction, there is still a great amount of emphasis on teacher-guided discussion. It is important, because of the teacher-guided discussion, for the teacher to provide varied levels of questioning.

FIGURE 1-4 Example of a Demonstration Lesson

Teacher: Ms. Davis   **Subject:** Social Studies

Grade: 4th   **Lesson Topic:** Items used by pioneers

Grouping Strategy (Predominant): Whole Group

Objectives: The students will be able to recognize the many different types of items used by the
   pioneers during everyday life.

INSTRUCTIONAL PROCEDURES:	MATERIALS:
1. Set up several displays containing items used for daily life in pioneer days.	Items from pioneer days: iron, skillet, lamps, washboard, etc.
2. Have the students sit on a circle on the floor.	
3. Show one item at a time and have the students guess what it is and why it was used.	
4. Explain to the students how the items were used during pioneer days.	
5. Ask the students how these items would compare to those of the present.	
6. After showing the items that were used for cooking, tell the students to imagine they are early pioneers and they need to prepare some food. Explain to the students that, along with some other foods, they may prepare some butter to eat with meals.	
7. Demonstrate to the students how to make butter by shaking whipping cream in a jar until butter mixture is formed. (Place in refrigerator overnight until hardened.)	jar whipping cream
8. Ask students to list items used by pioneers in their notebook.	notebook

EVALUATION:

STUDENT: The students will be evaluated through participation and by the list of items in their
       notebook.

TEACHER: Were the students interested in the lesson? Did they participate? Were they able to list
       a number of items in their notebook?

   Teacher questioning strategies have been the focus of a number of
studies (Guszak, 1967; Durkin, 1978–1979; Mehran, 1979; Heath, 1982;
Goodlad, 1984; Gillotte, 1991). The results from these and other studies
have indicated that a large amount of instructional time involves teachers
asking and receiving answers to literal questions. The frightening finding
is that 90% of these literal questions are answered correctly, which leads
to the conclusion that teachers limit the development of higher-order

---

TABLE 1-2 Levels of Questioning

Start out with basic knowledge questions and move up the levels. Then use a variety, going back and forth, depending on the topic and ability levels of the students.

Evaluation: Give the specifics of the problem and then an analysis of the solution, compare and contrast

Synthesis: Use creativity in your answer

Analysis: How does it all work together

Application: Who can apply, what should we do

Comprehension: What does it mean, can you tell us in your own words

Basic Knowledge: What, Who, How – Basic Recall

Start here

---

thinking skills by students. In the defense of teachers, the use (or overuse) of literal questions in some situations may be because they may not get to the point in the lesson where they are using higher-level questioning strategies. Unfortunately, in other situations, the teacher may not know how to ask higher-level questions.

In order to provide varied levels of questions, teachers need to make a conscious effort to use literal questions only as needed for development of student basic understanding. That is, questions should be hierarchical and lead students to think independently. While Bloom's taxonomy for questioning may be quite old, it is still an effective guide that teachers may follow in developing questions (Bloom, 1956). As described in Table 1-2, questions should be carefully formulated and should move from basic knowledge to higher-level evaluation. With experience in use of varied questioning strategies, teachers and students should be able to develop questions during ongoing discussions.

Another teacher-guided lesson that provides for a great deal of student/teacher interaction is semantic mapping. While in this strategy the teacher preselects the information to be studied, the objectives to be hoped for, and the general materials to be used, semantic mapping differs from the strategies previously discussed in that there is a greater amount of student input in the direction of the lesson that has an influence on the time frame for the lesson.

In semantic mapping there are basically four steps:

1. The teacher introduces the information and writes the key term on the board or overhead.
2. The teacher guides the thought processes of the students by asking key multilevel questions.
3. The students respond to the questions and their answers are recorded on the chart.
4. An appropriate follow-up activity is assigned by the teacher for completion by the students. (See Figure 1-5.)

Because of the amount of interaction that takes place in using a strategy such as semantic mapping, it is important that prior to implementation a teacher be aware of his level of tolerance for noise and ambiguity. It is equally important that the students in the class be prepared for their role in the lesson. Rules for discussion should be established prior to undertaking a lesson in which the students are active participants. A few simple rules that might be posted, and later referred to when beginning a lesson which requires discussion, could be similar to the following:

1. Listen attentively when others are speaking.
2. Be considerate of others' viewpoints and feelings.
3. Speak loudly and clearly enough for everyone to hear.
4. Let everyone have a turn.
5. Use facts to back up statements.

Basically, in using semantic mapping, or any other strategy where there is a great deal of interaction, the goal is to help students understand that through the discussion they are pooling their knowledge and that no one single student knows all the answers. Help them to understand that their pooled knowledge of information, ideas, and feelings is equally important.

A final teacher-guided lesson strategy to be discussed is the directed learning activity (DLA). Because social studies is a content area, it follows that a certain number of terms will be area specific. In addition, because social studies deals with an integration of facts and subjective interpretation, it is important that we help students develop skills in reading and

FIGURE 1-5 Example of Semantic Mapping

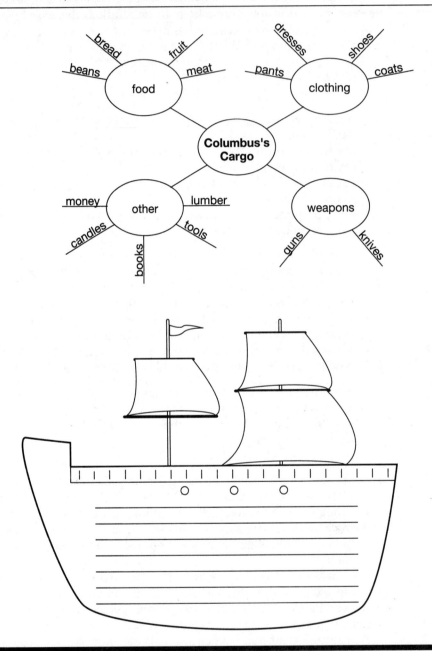

critically interpreting information. Cheek and Cheek developed a six-step plan for the DLA (Cheek & Cheek, 1983, p. 147). These steps include:

1. Introduction of vocabulary
2. Reading skill instruction or review
3. Prereading exercises
4. Reading of material
5. Teacher-guided discussion
6. Enrichment/reinforcement or review

These steps are sequential and, if followed carefully, should help students learn the information they are expected to read.

As with other strategies, in planning the DLA the teacher preselects the information to be studied, decides on the objectives to be achieved, selects the types and amount of material to be used during instruction, and decides on the time frame for the lesson. There is a certain amount of interaction which takes place in the DLA; however, the teacher guides or leads the students' interaction, especially until experience is gained in following discussion rules.

One component of the DLA, which is an extremely important part of the lesson, is the introduction of vocabulary. In order for students to learn

FIGURE 1-6 Suggested Steps for a Directed Learning Activity (DLA)

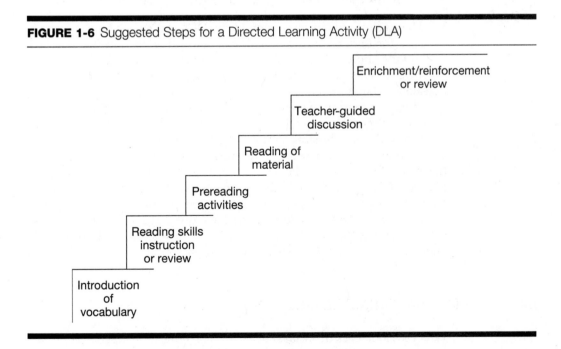

new information effectively, teachers must learn about the prior knowledge of the students. The time spent on finding out about the prior knowledge of students and on helping students to become familiar with new vocabulary is important to future learning because learning builds on previous knowledge. The easiest way for teachers to find out about the prior knowledge students might have is to ask a series of short questions.

Two other components of the DLA which are very important are reading and discussion. Reading is the basis for all instruction. In social studies, where a great deal of emphasis at the elementary and middle school levels is on the information in textbooks or printed resource materials, those students who do not have a solid foundation in reading skills will undoubtedly become frustrated learners or, in some unfortunate situations, nonlearners. While instructional time is limited, skills can be reviewed or introduced from time to time and will be beneficial for students as they study in all subject areas.

Reading skills that can be of great advantage for elementary and middle school students include:

1. Teaching new vocabulary as labels for concrete experiences and examples
2. Context clues: semantic and syntactic
3. Word association: relating prior knowledge to new information

The teacher-guided discussion in the DLA is a means for the teacher to check for understanding by students as well as to lead the students in thinking more critically about material they may encounter. Questions the teacher uses should progress from low-level factual types of questions related to the specific information being read to open-ended questions that encourage students to think about their responses and to be more reflective in answering.

Lastly, the enrichment/reinforcement or review portion of the lesson is important for the teacher and the students. It is not just a follow up on the lesson, but a time for the teacher to check again for understanding on the part of the students. It is also a time when the students may demonstrate their new knowledge either through discussion or by some written means. If it is found that the students have not, in general, been successful in attaining the objectives, the teacher may reteach the lesson using another strategy that she feels will help the students.

LEARNER INVOLVEMENT LESSONS

When we look back at social studies from an educational perspective, we see that historically if students were having any amount of enjoyment from instruction or learning experiences, the strategies being used were inappropriate or at least not intellectually stimulating. Learning, from a traditional viewpoint, should be in concert with structure and discipline. While it is imperative that teachers use strategies that they find comfortable, or easy to implement, it is equally important that teachers, whether novice or experienced, be willing to try or retry strategies which might be more conducive to helping students learn.

A key component of any learner involvement lesson, beyond the obvious related to content, is patience and understanding on the part of the teacher in implementation. Too many times we become frustrated with the seeming lack of cooperation by students when in reality they need time to be able to assimilate the expectations we have into their realm of everyday understanding in order to complete the task. The introduction of a new or not-very-familiar strategy can be compared to learning to drive a standard-shift vehicle, that is, it takes more than one try. The rule of thumb is to give any new instructional technique up to a week to begin to work, and then to rethink and try again at a later date.

Given this background, what is meant by the term learner involvement lesson? One might envision a classroom where the students are working in small groups or in pairs on given projects. Others might envision a whole class lesson where the interaction is initiated by the teacher, but the discussion is student centered. And finally, there may be those less than adventurous souls who may envision total chaos with little if any true learning taking place. For all of those scenarios described, the definition for learner involvement lessons is simply any type of learning experience provided in a stimulating environment in which students are at the center of the experience as active, knowledgeable, and willful participants.

The key factor in any learner involvement lesson is the teacher. The teacher must be highly aware of the natural curiosity of students. He must also be familiar with the interests of the students and use those interests as a sounding board or springboard for planning. In addition, the teacher must be open to having students raise questions and to suggest ways of completing a task. In essence, learner involvement lessons require a teacher to be comfortable with the idea that students are capable of taking responsibility for learning, if only given the opportunity.

Activity-based lessons are those that expand and increase knowledge about some aspect of the subject, topic, or concept being studied. In activity lessons, the teacher preselects the topics to be studied, decides on the objectives, selects the types of activities to be undertaken by the students, and plans the general time frame for the lesson. In choosing an activity for social studies, the teacher should consider many different aspects about the usefulness and appropriateness of the activity. Questions the teacher might use as guidelines include:

1. Is the activity within the students' abilities?
2. Is the activity useful and directly related to the objective?
3. Will students be involved in critical thinking and planning strategies as a part of the activity?
4. Are the materials needed for the activity readily available?

If the teacher is able to answer each of these questions in a positive way, then it is likely that the activity will aid in student learning.

Because of the involvement of students in activity-based lessons, it is important that students be familiarized with their roles and responsibilities prior to the introduction or beginning of the lesson. Students need to be able to recognize the purpose of the activity as it relates to the information being studied. While making butter may be a fun activity, students need to be aware of how the activity relates to the information they may be studying about pioneers. One of the more effective ways of insuring the recognition of the relationship between the activity and the objective is to include students in the planning process.

Students should also be involved in the closure of an activity lesson. Questions, which may provide an evaluation for the teacher, should be raised and addressed. If an activity lesson will last for more than one class period (i.e., more than one day), the teacher needs to help students make plans for the next meeting and evaluate how well the students worked together and how the lesson might be improved.

Another type of learner involvement lesson in which it is equally important that students understand their role in completing tasks is that of cooperative learning. One of the goals of social studies instruction is to help students learn social and life skills. Cooperative learning is an effective and appropriate method for providing students with opportunities in social and life skills. In addition, cooperative learning strategies help students learn how to work with others who may be different, that is, not only different culturally, but by possible physical or capability differences.

In using cooperative learning, the teacher needs first to consider the topic to be studied, the objectives, the types of materials needed to complete the study, and the time frame in which the students will be working on a particular study. With this information in hand, the teacher has the task of assigning goals for particular groups and organizing the makeup of the groups.

In deciding on students to be grouped together, there are a number of factors that need to be considered. According to Cohen (1986), one extremely important factor is to avoid placing friends in the same group. When friends are grouped together, more play than work is accomplished. Another factor to be considered is the need to mix varying ability and social skills levels within a group.

TABLE 1-3 General Interest Inventory

Investigating Children's Interests

---

1. What do you like to do when you get home from school?
2. What do you like to do on Saturday?
3. Do you like to watch television?
   If you do, what are the names of your favorite programs?
4. Do you have a hobby?
   If you do, what is your hobby?
5. Do you like to make or collect things?
   If you do, what have you made or collected?
6. What is your favorite sport?
7. What games do you like best?
8. Do you like to go to the movies?
   If you do, what is your favorite movie?
9. Do you have a pet?
10. Where have you spent your summer vacation?
11. Have you ever made a special study?

rocks	space
plants	animals
travel	dinosaurs
other	

12. What are your favorite subjects in school?

art	handwriting
social studies	reading
physical education	science
spelling	arithmetic
creative writing	English
other	

13. What subject is hardest for you?
    Easiest for you?
14. What kinds of books do you like to read?

animal stories	picture books
fairy tales	true stories
science fiction	adventures
mysteries	sport stories
poems	funny stories
other kinds of stories	

The roles various students may hold within a group structure also needs to be considered. It is important that all students be given opportunities to be a group leader. Because the teacher is responsible for the objectives of each group, she should keep searching for objectives that can serve academic needs while using the special talents of each student in the

TABLE 1-4 Phases of the Jigsaw Method

Phase 1	Teacher presents home group with general information.
Phase 2	Expert groups meet to explore specific assignments.
Phase 3	Home groups meet to discuss and instruct one another about specific assignments.
Phase 4	Individual students are evaluated on specific and general information.

class. Although this may sound impossible, if we stop to consider the number of lessons we have in social studies during a given academic year, it becomes more feasible.

While there are numerous variations or strategies of cooperative learning which may be appropriately used as a part of social studies instruction, such as STAD (student teams achievement division), structured controversy, group investigation, and circles of learning, the discussion will be limited to the jigsaw method (Aronson, 1978; Cohen, 1986; Slavin, 1986). In the jigsaw method, students are members of two groups with each group being limited to four or five students; one is the home group and the other is the expert group (Aronson, 1978).

In planning the use of the jigsaw method, it is important to note that there are basically four phases of learning or instruction. After dividing the class into heterogeneous groups of four or five students, their home groups, the first phase should be undertaken. In this first phase, the home group covers the same general information. In this way the teacher can provide background information that may be necessary in order for students to carry out the individual activities of the following phases. In the second phase, individual assignments are made and all students with similar assignments meet with their expert group in order to explore more thoroughly the information related to the assignment. In this phase students seek out as much information as possible about their topic using available resources and materials. The third phase is when students meet back with their home group. In this phase, each group member teaches the rest of the group about his or her specific assignment. Finally, in the fourth phase, the group members are evaluated individually on the specific assignment as well as the group assignment.

Another type of learner involvement lesson which is exceptionally useful in social studies instruction is simulation. In social studies, some concepts or topics would be easier and better understood if the students were able to experience the actual situation. Since it is impossible, as well as impractical, for all actual events to be experienced by students, simulations can be designed or commercial simulations used that will enable students to act out a situation as closely as possible, leaving out any characteristics which might have harmful effects. For example, students can learn about the role of a judge and jury through a simulated court experience without actually being involved in an act that would lead to arrest and a trial.

The teacher's role in implementing the use of simulations includes preselecting the topic or focus of study, the objectives, the materials or resources to be used, and the time frame for the simulation. As with other learner involvement lessons, the teacher should be aware of the various abilities, interests, talents, and prior knowledge in giving assignments to the students. Also, it is very important that the teacher check the students' understanding of the goals and guidelines for the lesson prior to implementation. Students need to understand the importance of following the guidelines so that accurate representations can be made.

In a simulation, students are actively involved in promotion of a viewpoint, thought, or idea, or students may be involved in a problem-solving activity. It is important in the development of roles that students remain as accurate as possible in their portrayal of a person or in the presentation of facts. All directions and information about the role should be provided to the student in detail.

While there are a great number of commercial simulations available (Table 1-5), teachers may design their own to better meet the needs of a particular class. Family, economic, social, or historical issues are examples

TABLE 1-5 Commercial Simulations Sources and References

The Oregon Trail; The Market Place. Minnesota Educational Computing Consortium (MECC), 3490 Lexington Avenue North, St. Paul, MN 55126.

Decisions, Decisions; Choices, Choices; and *Our Town Meeting.* Tom Snyder Productions, 123 Auburn Street, Cambridge, MA 02138.

Stock Market. Learning Arts, P.O. Box 179, Wichita, KS 67201.

INTERACT, P.O. Box 997-S90, Lakeside, CA 92940

Social Studies School Service, P.O. Box 802, Culver City, CA 90232

Arnold, J. (1990). *Visions of teaching and learning: 80 exemplary middle level projects.* Columbus, OH: National Middle School Association.

Heitzmann, W. R. (1987). *Educational games and simulations.* Washington, DC: National Education Association.

Jones, K. (1985). *Designing your own simulations.* New York: Methuen.

Muir, S. P. (1980). Simulation games for elementary social studies. *Social Education, 44,* 35–39, 76.

Wentworth, D. R., & Lewis, D. R. (1973). A review of research on instructional games and simulations in social studies education. *Social Education, 37,* 437–448.

of areas that might be addressed in a simulation. It is important in selecting or designing a simulation to keep the maturity level of the students in mind in addition to the academic needs. Some programs that are designed for upper elementary may be useful for middle school students as well; however, the use of these materials may not be appropriate for lower elementary levels. Teachers working with lower elementary levels or with students who may not be on grade level will find it helpful to preview material carefully for usefulness and appropriateness.

A final learner involvement strategy to be discussed is individualized instruction. While those of us who have been a part of the educational arena for a while have often heard this phrase, there have been only a courageous few who have actually implemented the technique with continuous success. In education, we are becoming more aware of the differences among students due to the recognition in our country of pluralism, diversity, and multicultural influences. In addition, we are increasingly becoming aware of the ways students differ in areas more specifically related to academic success. Among these areas are student differences in background experiences, motivation to learn, rate of learning, ability to learn, and learning styles. Given this information, along with the knowledge that students need experiences that are meaningful in order for learning to take place, individualized instruction is a logical strategy for helping students achieve learning goals.

First it needs to be made clear that while the phrase individualized instruction may bring to mind a one-on-one tutorial setting, in fact, this is an erroneous idea. Individualized instruction occurs when each student has the opportunity to experience learning that focuses on the most suitable techniques being implemented based on his or her educational needs and capabilities. While all students may have varying specific needs and capabilities, usually in a heterogeneously grouped class, there will be a number of students who have many similarities. Because of this, teachers may use learner groups in order to individualize instruction more effectively and efficiently.

The teacher has a number of responsibilities to undertake in planning for individualized instruction in addition to the understood academic planning. First, the physical environment of the classroom has to be arranged in a student-centered manner. This, of course, means students need to have easy access to materials such as books, computers, and other media. In addition, desks need to be arranged in ways that encourage interaction as opposed to traditional straight rows, which tend to suppress interaction. (See Figure 1-7.) A second responsibility of the teacher deals with grouping students for instruction in ways that will be most effective. In the area of social studies, these groups should be temporary or constantly having a change in membership depending on the topic

FIGURE 1-7 Classroom Floor Plan for Individualized Instruction

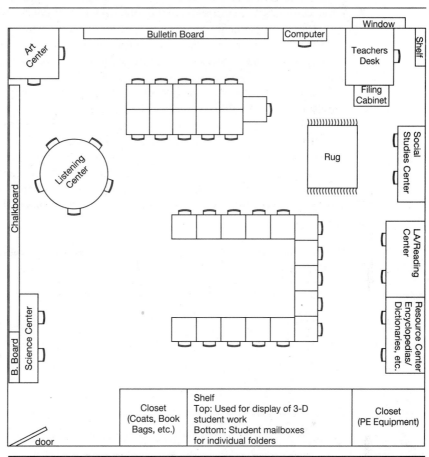

being studied. As with jigsaw, teachers need to select students carefully when organizing groups to avoid management problems. A third area the teacher needs to plan carefully prior to implementation is scheduling. It is important to keep in mind the variations in time required by students to complete a given study; however, it is equally important that students be made aware of the time requirements so that all students will complete the assignment.

In planning individualized instruction, the teacher preselects the materials to be used, the objectives, the time frame for the work to be completed, and, of course, the topic to be studied. The teacher may develop a learning contract according to his style of teaching and taking the level of the student into consideration. While the specific objectives that are to be met and lists of materials may be attached, the actual contract needs to be written at the vocabulary level of the student so that it can be easily understood by the student. Each student may complete a contract prepared by the teacher as a part of the lesson. By using a contract, students within a given group may have specific assignments that relate to their special needs, interests, or talents, while still being responsible for information that is being covered by all students in their group.

The use of the contract as a part of individualized instruction in social studies is especially helpful for teachers who may have a class with a number of exceptional students, that is, any students with needs beyond those of the norm (i.e., often referred to as Special Education Students, who may be labeled with any combination of letters from EMR to AP). It is very important that the teacher be aware of the special needs of these

FIGURE 1-8 Learning Contract for Individualized Instruction

Social Studies Learning Contract

I, _____, hereby agree to do the following activities in Social Studies:

Activity   Date due

1. _____   _____
   _____
   _____

2. _____   _____
   _____
   _____

3. _____   _____
   _____
   _____

_____
Student's signature

_____
Teacher's signature

_____
Today's date

students and plan with colleagues so that appropriate information can be provided for optimal learning.

As with other learner involvement lessons, the teacher needs to be aware of her willingness or openness to ambiguity, flexibility, noise, and movement. All of these are factors that come into play in implementing individualized instruction. Patience is an imperative quality that the teacher must have until students become familiar with the system of individualized instruction. As with discussion groups or other student-centered activities, students need to be informed of the guidelines they are to follow. These guidelines should be posted so that, if needed, students can refer to them as they work on their projects.

USING RESOURCES IN SOCIAL STUDIES

Sadly, too many times the main source and tool used for instruction in social studies is the textbook. Other than the textbook, encyclopedias are the second main source for social studies instruction. The shortage of funds which has forced cutbacks in many areas of public education has likewise been labeled as the culprit leading to fewer materials being used in social studies instruction. However, creative, inventive, and willing teachers seek out resources so that students can continue to receive quality instruction even under financially strained circumstances.

First, the teacher needs to identify areas in which he feels instructional enrichment would be helpful beyond the information on hand. A "wish-list" of sorts may be developed so that as need arises, resources will be more available. Working with colleagues and forming a grade level unit list of resources will help to develop a more complete list. The list may also be divided into two main sections; that is, one list of printed or film/slide/video resources and one list of persons to contact as speakers in a variety of areas. The list may further be divided between the information that may be obtained through national organizations, cooperations, and government agencies, and information obtained through local sources.

The national list might include some of the following sources for information:

National Council for the Social Studies
3501 Newark Street NW
Washington, DC 20016

American Bar Association
1155 E 60th Street
Chicago, IL 60637

Minnesota Educational Computing
 Consortium
3490 Lexington Ave. North
St. Paul, MN 55126

Social Science Education Consortium
855 Broadway
Boulder, CO 80302

American Newspaper Publishers
   Association Foundation
Box 17407
Dulles International Airport
Washington, DC 20041

In addition, primary sources may become a part of the resources used in social studies instruction. Primary sources are firsthand accounts of events. Also included as primary sources are documents. The term document usually brings to mind such significant statements as the *Declaration of Independence,* the *U.S. Constitution,* or the *Gettysburg Address;* however, local community charters, family documents, and bylaws of organizations are also documents which may be useful in various social studies activities.

While there are various reasons for using primary sources as a part of social studies instruction, the basic reason is to gather information about the particular source and relate it to the topic being studied. Questions that might be used when using primary sources include:

- Who was involved in writing the document?
- When and why was it written?
- Is it a legal binding document?
- Why has this document been saved for others to see?
- Is the document fair (in terms of cultural application)?

For primary sources that are not documents, questions might include:

- What does this source help me to understand?
- Who is responsible for the information?
- What is the purpose?

The following list provides suggestions concerning locating primary sources:

Local government offices	Individual businesses
Community organizations	Local museums
National, state or local historical organizations	Diaries
	Letters
Photographs	Books
Estate sales	

A general list of local resources that may supply guest speakers in addition to materials might include:

Local TV/radio stations	Utility companies
Local newspapers	Local law enforcement agencies
Universities/colleges within the area	Local courts
Museums, parks, zoos	Chamber of Commerce
Fire department	City council
Community library	Hospital/medical center
Red Cross	Post office
	Jr. Achievement

A number of untapped local resources that will be helpful in identifying guest speakers may also be developed. These sources might include:

Retirement/nursing homes	Other faculty/staff—from jr. high or high school
Video exchange clubs for educators	Missionary societies
Travel agencies	Local businesses—department stores, specialty stores, pet shops, grocery stores, factories, cabinet shops
Restaurant owners/staff	
Freelance journalists	
Freelance photographers	Humane society workers
Town/state welcome centers	Recycling centers
	Airport personnel
Train station personnel	Bus terminal personnel
Forestry service	Parents, grandparents

While this list may seem a little offbeat from the familiar, we need to encourage community involvement in our schools as often as possible. To give an example of how one finds resource people everywhere, in one of my college level classes, our temporary departmental secretary, who by training was actually a medical laboratory technician, brought in her spinning wheel, cotton from a nearby cotton field, angora rabbits, and wool from her llama to help students better understand the reasons pioneers were careful with their clothing and the hardships they must have encountered in transporting a spinning wheel. Needless to say, this made a lasting impression on the students. She became somewhat of a regular in the classes where they were completing internships and later recommended a number of her friends in the spinning club as resource speakers.

As lists are compiled for resource speakers, guidelines for presentations might also be developed so that resource speakers will be more at

TABLE 1-6 Guidelines for Resource Speakers

Do	Don't
Consider the ages and experiences of students. Prepare yourself adequately. Encourage active participation by students. Relax and be yourself. Use a variety of teaching strategies during your visit. Discuss them with the teacher before your visit. Be a question-asker, not just an answer-provider. Involve the teacher in the lesson as needed. Prepare for this in advance. Try to contact the teacher after your visit. Ask for a sincere, candid evaluation of your presentation. This is the best way to improve your presentations.	Schedule visits for times when a cancellation is in any way foreseeable. Lecture at students. Use jargon or unfamiliar words without explaining them. Read a prepared speech. Be afraid not to have an answer at your fingertips. If you need to research a question for the class, don't forget to do so. Be too esoteric. Put yourself in the students' shoes. Overdress.

ease about visiting the class as well as more prepared. (See Table 1-6.) Specific information should be given to the resource person when she has been contacted about a presentation. This information should include:

1. The goals and objectives of the unit being taught and what contributions the resource person can make.
2. What students will be studying before and after the visit. This will help the resource person to plan more effectively. Also, the teacher should ask if there is any specific information the students need as preparation for the resource person's visit.
3. Class size and general ability levels.
4. Date, time, and exact location. Parking information as well as the location of the office would be of great value to a resource person not familiar with the school.
5. Phone numbers. The teacher's home phone would be helpful, as well as the school office number in the event of a cancellation or an emergency (e.g., a flat tire on the way to the school).
6. Confirmation letter or call. Most resource speakers will not need a reminder; however, it is only appropriate and wise on the part of the teacher to check a day or two before the presentation for any last minute changes or preparations that might need to be made.

It is vital that the class be prepared for the visit. They should be aware of the purpose of the visit, the expectations you have concerning what they should learn, and guidelines they should follow concerning participation. Also, on the day of the visit, it would be most helpful for the students to have name tags.

As a part of the visit followup, the students might write brief thank-you notes. These should be sent to the resource speaker along with a formal letter of appreciation from the teacher. If the resource speaker had to have permission to leave work in order to visit, or if someone asked them to come as a representative of their organization, if possible an appreciation letter should also be sent to the supervising person.

Again, resources are available from a variety of sources to enrich the study of almost any topic in social studies. It is important that teachers be willing to seek out these resources and make them part of instruction.

BULLETIN BOARDS IN SOCIAL STUDIES

Envision two classrooms. In one, there is a bulletin board the length of one wall with divisions for the various content areas. In each space there are appropriate titles and attractive displays of teacher-made or purchased information related to the content areas. In the second classroom, there is a similar board with divisions and appropriate titles but rather than displays on every board, several include manipulative or interactive activities. Also in the second classroom, no space is wasted which might be used for display of student work.

In thinking about bulletin boards, the two types most prevalent are those described in the classrooms above; that is, the display and the interactive bulletin boards. The display may be for decoration, announcements, management, or student work. The interactive may be used as a type of learning center, a reinforcement of information that is being covered, enrichment about topics of study or interest, and a springboard of thoughts or questions to encourage critical thinking or self-concept development. Either type of board may be appropriate, depending on the purpose or goal. (See Figure 1-9.)

One of the main concerns of teachers in developing bulletin boards is space. Most elementary classrooms will have at least one stationary bulletin board; however, portable bulletin boards of various sizes may be used if needed. Walls, closet doors, or the classroom door itself may also be transformed into bulletin boards. Portable bulletin boards may be the commercial type, or may be made from foam core, insulation, or an opened corrugated cardboard box.

Regardless of the type or purpose of the board, there are a few basic guidelines teachers might consider in planning a board so that it will be attractive and convey the message intended. Neatness is probably one of the most important factors in developing a bulletin board. Letters should be uniform and if cut out, done neatly so that words are easily read. In selecting the type of letters to be used, grade level consideration should be given. Letters may be made from a variety of materials in addition

FIGURE 1-9 Example of a Portable Interactive Bulletin Board

Game: The student starts at the upper right-hand corner and travels west (left) by successfully answering questions listed on the green (lower level) and red (upper level) cards. The pictures along the edges of the board are related to the questions.

Puppets: Paper bag puppets may be made by the students to use in skits or group question and answer sessions.

Design a Quilt: Pre-cut fabric triangles are glued on to pieces of paper to form a "quilt." Since some quilts are designed to tell a story, students may write a story to accompany their quilt.

Live and Learn With Pioneers: Cards and pictures can provide facts about experiences had by Pioneers during their travels throughout the West. Students use these facts as the basis for stories written from the perspective of a boy or girl of their age who traveled during the Westward Expansion Movement.

to construction paper. Newspaper, book jackets, or colorful shopping bags are suggestions. A variety of materials may also be used for the background. Fabric, old window curtains, shower curtains, trash bags, thin carpet or floor coverings all make interesting backgrounds.

Color for the background, border, and letters should be eye-catching but not harsh or faded-out. In selecting the colors to be used, consideration needs to be given to the size of the board, the lighting in the room, the location of the board within the room, and the type of board (display or interactive).

The organization of material on the bulletin board is also a factor that must be considered if a quality board is to be developed. Simplicity is the rule of thumb with unnecessary information being left off the board. Too much information on a board will distract from its usefulness.

One additional factor that teachers may need to be reminded of is time. The usefulness of a board will depend on the topic, how it is being referred to in class instruction or discussion, and the type of board (display or interactive). If the students are no longer gaining knowledge from the board, or if it is providing outdated information (e.g., student work, management, announcements), it needs to be changed.

CURRENT AFFAIRS IN SOCIAL STUDIES

Friday was always current affairs day. We had to bring in a clipping from the newspaper glued on a sheet of notebook paper. It really didn't matter what it was, as long as we had one. Since my family didn't take a paper, this always involved going to a neighbor and asking for the paper, not an easy task for us rural students. Later, as a teacher, I saw the assignment was equally frustrating for some of the inner-city and suburban students. Perhaps the students' frustration, which leads to magnified frustration for the teacher, is one reason the area of current affairs as a part of social studies is neglected to a great extent.

Since one of the goals in social studies is to help students develop skills needed to become productive citizens in a changing world, it should follow that current affairs instruction is an appropriate and important means of providing experiences in dealing with the realities of an ever changing world. While there are a number of methods for including current affairs instruction, the most common method is that of teaching current affairs in addition to social studies.

In teaching current affairs in addition to regular social studies, the focus of instruction may or may not be directly related to the topics being studied. The goal is to build interest of students in becoming knowledgeable about events in their surroundings on a local, national, and worldwide level. A second goal is to help students develop critical thinking and interpretive skills. A third factor in teaching current affairs, especially if in a great portion of instruction the students are working with printed materials, is the focus on reading skills.

When implementing the use of current affairs instruction, there are certain factors the teacher needs to consider. First, guidelines for instruction must be developed. Guidelines should be formulated considering the

---

FIGURE 1-10 Letter to Parents or Guardians

Dear _____ ,

   The students in our class will be completing an assignment in current affairs. The assignment is:

_____

_____

_____

_____

_____

_____

_____

_____

   The assignment is due on _____

_____ .

If you have any questions about the assignment, or need help so that your child can complete the assignment, please let me know by _____ .

Thank you for your help.

Sincerely,

---

school community. Topics that may be appropriate in one locality may be extremely controversial in others. Teachers should use their own mature professional judgement in considering acceptable topics and reserve the right to deem some topics inappropriate. Also in planning guidelines, the teacher should consider the general maturation and ability levels of the students. The types of assignments will differ for younger and older students (i.e., more general for younger and more specific for older students).

   It is important that parents or guardians be notified of the types of assignments being made in current affairs. The reason for this is simply that not all students have access to sources for such assignments. Some students may be limited in the amount of time they are able to watch TV per week, and school assignments will most likely be in addition to their allotted time. Also, not all homes have a daily paper, so arrangements will need to be made. If students are required to watch a specific news program or have a printed article on a particular day, the teacher should provide access to students if this is not possible at home.

As mentioned, current affairs instruction is not limited to newspaper articles. In the ever-advancing technological world, a variety of sources are available, however, the two still most common are radio and television. While regular AM/FM radio news programs are generally limited to brief summaries of news once per hour, these can prove helpful in providing students with highlights of issues that may be of interest, especially on a local level. Television news, other than cable stations devoted entirely to news, is more detailed and is generally divided among topics of local, national, and worldwide interest. Both of these sources for current affairs require active participation by students. These sources, however, may prove difficult to work with in some situations because some students may need to be taught listening skills prior to being given a particular assignment. Also, it would be beneficial for the teacher to make audiotapes or videotapes of a number of programs in advance of assigning such current affairs sources. This will help students become more aware of how to listen and take notes, not just "kind-of" listen as they do some other activity.

In order to help students become better listeners, the teacher needs to set the purpose for listening; that is, provide a means of focusing student attention. For example, in listening to a news broadcast, students might be listening for news about a specific person or event. This would require the student to stay focused throughout the rest of the broadcast until the person or event is mentioned. (For more on listening, see Unit 4.)

Students also need to be guided in methods of taking notes. One downfall of many elementary and middle school, and sometimes even college students, is that they attempt to write down everything that is being said. Students need to focus on writing down only the information needed to share effectively with others. For example, students might be asked to answer the "5 Ws and How with summary." (See Figure 1-11.)

FIGURE 1-11 5 Ws and How Plus Summary

WHO	(Person[s])
WHEN	(Time, date)
WHERE	(Place)
WHAT	(The main event)
WHY	(Why did it happen or why is it important)
HOW	(How did it happen)
SUMMARY	(Write a one or two sentence summary of the information in your own words)

This will help them to organize the information they have heard. By developing a summary statement (i.e., a sentence or two, as appropriate) using their own words, the students will be able to use what they have heard and not just listen for the sake of listening.

As with many other traditional strategies and materials used as a part of social studies instruction, the newspaper as a main source for current affairs instruction has improved over a number of years. Guidelines and suggestions for the use of newspapers in classroom settings are provided by the American Newspaper Publishers Association Foundation (116007 Sunrise Valley Dr., Reston, VA 22091) in the Newspaper in Education program. In addition, student periodicals have improved to be more factual and updated. Two examples are *Weekly Reader* and *Scholastic*.

Scholastic Inc.	*Weekly Reader*
P.O. Box 3710	4343 Equity Drive
Jefferson City, MO 65102	Columbus, OH 43216

In addition to student periodicals, these publications have accompanying teachers' editions and resource materials to help in using the information as learning tools (e.g., maps, pictures, transparencies or black-line masters for making transparencies).

A number of activities can be implemented in the area of current affairs instruction. A special bulletin board should be maintained for display of the students' articles. Not only may the printed materials be posted, but student summaries, thoughts, or reactions may be placed near a given article. In using national or international information, an accompanying map with the location of the related area highlighted will help students develop more understanding of geographic information.

In helping elementary and middle school students understand the background behind news stories, local TV and radio personalities may be invited to meet with students or, if possible, the students may visit the local station. It would also be quite interesting for a local newspaper reporter to speak to the class about how news stories are investigated, written, and finally published.

While visiting a newsroom or by having an appropriate guest speaker, students are exposed to the amount and types of work (e.g., investigation) that is required prior to a story being aired. The emphasis on accuracy will help students become better listeners when later watching and listening to a news broadcast. In addition, with the popularity of amateur home videos being used in news stories, one exciting learning experience for students is to provide them with the opportunity to develop a news story, from beginning to end. Again, this will emphasize the importance on several levels of being accurate.

SUMMARY

While Unit 1 has a great deal of information, it is hoped that the intent has not been lost. In each area, examples and suggestions have been given to encourage novice teachers to be willing to attempt variety in instructional techniques. At the same time, it is hoped that those classroom practitioners viewing this work have been "fired-up" and are now willing to try or retry certain strategies.

Cooperative learning, demonstration lessons, interactive bulletin boards, and using the video camera in teaching current affairs are just a few of the areas discussed. We must face the reality that change is a necessity in working with students, whether that change means our own way of thinking or a strategy we use because it is comfortable or easy. Social studies is not a static content area; therefore, change is a natural part of the content and can most easily become a part of the instruction.

HELPFUL HINTS FOR UNIT 1:

1. In looking back at your school experiences, what do you remember about social studies? How do you want your students to remember social studies?

2. Develop an outline for an ideal social studies curriculum. Compare your plans with a partner. Compare your plans with those suggested in Unit 1.

3. Look carefully at the lesson plans in Unit 1. Which one would you like to implement? Why?

4. Select a broad topic that you are familiar with in the area of social studies. Develop a semantic map on the topic. Remember, simplicity and creativity are important.

5. Visit the local curriculum or teachers resource center. Locate and review a commercial simulation. Be prepared to share your thoughts with your group.

6. Develop a list of ten local resources that you might use in teaching social studies. Compare and combine your list with those of your peers.

7. Design, sketch, and provide a written description of a display and interactive bulletin board. Be sure to explain when and why each would be appropriate.

8. Cut out two articles from the local newspaper. Develop a plan for using the article in a social studies lesson.

REFERENCES

Aronson, E. (1978). *The jigsaw classroom.* Beverly Hills, CA: Sage.

Barnard, J. (1913). The teaching of civics in elementary and secondary schools. *Journal of the Fifty First Convention of the National Education Association, 50,* 84–90.

Baskerville, R. & Sesow, F. (1976). In defense of Hanna and the "expanding environments" approach to social studies. *Theory and Research in Social Education, 4,* 1, 20–32.

Bloom, B. (Ed.). (1956). *Taxonomy of educational objectives. Handbook I: Cognitive Domain.* New York: David McKay.

Chapin, J. R. & Messick. R. G. (1992). *Elementary social studies: A practical guide.* New York: Longman.

Cheek, E. H. & Cheek, M. C. (1983). *Reading instruction through content teaching.* Columbus, OH: Merrill Publishing Company.

Cohen, E. G. (1986). *Designing group work.* New York: Teachers College Press.

Croswell, T. R. (1897). Courses of study in the elementary schools of the United States. *The Pedagogical Seminary, 4,* 295–335.

Durkin, D. (1978–1979). What classroom observations reveal about reading comprehension instruction. *Reading Research Quarterly, 14,* 481–533.

Gillotte, H. (1991, April). *The examination of literature-based series: Potential problems for minority students.* Paper presented at the annual meeting of the American Educational Research Association, Chicago.

Goodlad, J. I. (1984). *A place called school.* New York: McGraw-Hill.

Guszak, F. J. (1967). Teacher questioning and reading. *Reading Teacher, 21,* 227–234.

Hall, G. S. (1901). The ideal school as based on child study. *Journal of the Proceedings and Addresses of the Fortieth Annual Meeting of the National Education Association, 39,* 474–490.

Heath, S. B. (1982). Questioning at home and at school: A comparative study. In G. Spindler (Ed.), *Doing the ethnography of schooling: Educational anthropology in action* (pp. 102–131). New York: Holt.

Jacobs, H. H. (1989). The growing need for interdisciplinary curriculum content. In H. H. Jacobs (Ed.), *Interdisciplinary curriculum: Design and implementation* (pp. 1–12). Alexandria, VA: Association for Supervision and Curriculum Development.

Jarolimek, J. & Parker, W. C. (1993). *Social studies in elementary education.* New York: Macmillan.

Jones, R., Conner, W., Bardwell, R., Barnard, J., Binford, J., Knowlton, D., Senour, A., & Yawberg, A. (1926). The social studies. *Yearbook of the Department of Superintendence of the National Education Association, 4,* 323–378.

Joyce, W. & Alleman-Brooks, J. (1982). The child's world. *Social Education, 46,* 538–541.

Mehran, H. (1979). "What time is it, Denise?" Asking known information questions in classroom discourse. *Theory Into Practice, 18,* 285–294.

Morrissett, I. (1981). The needs of the future and the constraints of the past. In H. D. Mehlinger and O. L. Davis, Jr. (Eds.), *The social studies.* (80th Yearbook of the National Society for the Study of Education). Chicago: University of Chicago Press.

National Council for the Social Studies. (1990). *Social Studies Curriculum Planning Resources.* Dubuque, IA: Kendall/Hunt, 20.

Naylor, D. & Diem, Z. (1987). *Elementary and middle school social studies.* New York: Random House.

Ruddell, R. B. & Harris, P. (1991). A study of the relationship between influential teachers' prior knowledge and teaching effectiveness: Developing higher order thinking in content areas. In S. McCormick & J. Zutell (Eds.), *Cognition and Social Perspectives for Literacy Research and Instruction,* 38th Yearbook of the National Reading Conference (pp. 461–472). Chicago: NRC.

Slavin, R. E. (1986). *Using team learning.* Baltimore, MD: Johns Hopkins University.

Steele, R. (1911). Cliff dwellers and city dwellers in the third grade. *Teacher College Record, 12,* 25–39.

Sunal, C. S. (1990). *Early childhood social studies.* Columbus, OH: Merrill Publishing Company.

Superka, D. Hawke, S. & Morrissett, I. (1980). The current and future status of the social studies. *Social Education, 44,* (May), 362–369.

Taba, H. 1971. *Teacher's Handbook for Elementary Social Studies.* Menlo Park, CA: Addison-Wesley.

Wade, J. (1911). Harvest festival in kindergarten and grades. *Teacher College Record, 12,* 25–39.

1. Why do beginning teachers often rely on textbooks for social studies instruction? **2.** How do recent social studies content texts compare to those used 10 or 15 years ago? **3.** Define scope and sequence in terms of importance for social studies instruction. **4.** What components are generally part of a published social studies program? **5.** Is evaluation of materials a static aspect of instruction? Why or why not? **6.** Describe what you think is the best method for use of a published social studies program in elementary and middle school.

Social Studies Texts

INTRODUCTION One of the most important tools used for social studies instruction in many elementary and middle school classrooms is the textbook. The purpose of this section is to take a closer look at the general characteristics of published social studies programs. As a part of the discussion, a number of areas will be explored, such as content, use, and evaluation of the text and resource materials. Each are looked at as a positive means for adding to social studies instruction, yet emphasis is placed on using the text as a basic resource rather than a means to an end in social studies instruction.

CHARACTERISTICS OF PUBLISHED PROGRAMS

When we stop to consider the textbooks used in social studies, invariably our thoughts return to memories of our own experiences at the elementary and middle school levels. More often than not, lessons which come to mind are related to certain map or geography lessons or pictures of national figures (e.g., historical persons), monuments (e.g., buildings, statues, landmarks) or holiday celebrations. If asked about the main instructional strategies employed using the published social studies program, a large portion of young adults would probably say "read and answer the questions at the end of the chapter."

If we compare a recent edition of a social studies textbook to those we had as elementary or middle school students, we would probably discover a number of differences. In addition, if we talked with our former elementary or middle school teachers about the program they used compared with those available today, we would probably be shocked!

While textbook series vary from publisher to publisher, there are a number of components that are usually found in every series. These are:

1. Student books
2. Teacher's edition/manual
3. Student workbooks
4. Teacher's edition of the student workbook
5. Tests
6. Duplicating and copying masters
7. Additional supplementary materials

It is important that we not only be aware of the materials generally found in published programs, but also that novice educators understand possible uses for the different materials.

Student books.   These books contain the bulk of information the students are expected to learn. Also included in the book are question sections, pictures, drawings, maps, and a glossary.

Teacher's edition of the text.   The teacher's edition includes the same information as the student text. In addition, a detailed set of directions or teaching plans are provided. Discussion questions to help guide instruction, along with correct or possible answers are usually provided. Also, often the teacher's edition will include suggestions for additional instructional or enrichment activities or children's literature that might be used as a reinforcement.

Student workbooks. The workbooks are designed as consumable materials for students to use. These usually contain activities related to the concepts, generalizations, and skills covered in the particular program.

Teacher's edition of the student workbook. As with the book that is used, the teacher's edition is usually an exact copy of the student workbook along with additional directions and correct answers. Suggestions for discussion questions may also be provided.

Tests. While the format of the tests or evaluation instruments may vary between publishers, those most often included are unit tests and chapter tests. In some programs, skills tests are also provided.

Duplicating and copying masters. These are usually additional practice activities similar to those in the student workbook. Also, letters that teachers may send to parents or guardians are often included. These are especially useful because they provide a means for parental involvement in the social studies program.

Additional supplementary materials. Other materials that may be available to aid in social studies instruction include maps, slides, films, videos, charts, pictures, posters, and most recently, computer programs.

It is important to note that in some series, the teacher's manual, duplicating and copying masters, and other supplementary materials are the components available for kindergarten levels and for some lower or primary levels of the elementary school. These materials are designed to introduce very general concepts, skills, and generalizations.

The components of the published program are provided for the teacher as a resource or tool to use in helping students learn. While the materials provided by a publisher may be the same throughout the country, it is important that classroom practitioners use what they know about their students and then implement use of those materials that are most appropriate.

CONTENT OF SOCIAL STUDIES TEXTS

As mentioned before, a majority of us can probably look back at our experiences in elementary and middle school social studies and remember bits and pieces of information we encountered. As novice and experienced educators we must be aware of the content found in the texts we use. In addition, we need to look at the content and evaluate its appropriateness in relation to the needs of the students we work with on a daily basis.

One first area that educators would be wise to note is the method of presentation found in social studies textbooks. While most published social studies texts follow a prescribed scope (i.e., a set of particular concepts, generalizations, skills, and information) and sequence (i.e., the order in which the scope is presented), it is important that we remember that a group of authors and editors were involved in the actual content provided; therefore, the views of those persons may have contributed to the types and amount of information included in the text (Hooper & Smith, 1993). Given this, it is important for educators to check the content provided for bias or viewpoints that do not align with those of the school community, or for the grade level and maturity level of the students.

Most educators would agree that the overall content included in textbooks has improved over a period of years. Information is presented in well-planned organization that reflects an understanding, by the publishers, of the types and amounts of information needed by students at the elementary and middle school grade levels. This includes the area of technical vocabulary, the vocabulary particular to the area of social studies; visual stimuli, the types and number of photographs, charts, and graphs related to the information being provided; and structure or literary quality, that is, the length of sentences and paragraphs is based on what is generally accepted as being appropriate for given grade levels.

In considering the content of textbooks or more specifically, the structure or writing style of the text, it is important for educators to consider the relationship between the style and the effects it has on students. In the primary grade levels, information is generally written in a narrative or story-like style or format. Because students in the primary grades are more familiar with this style of writing from published reading programs as well as children's literature, it is easier for them to understand. Usually around third or fourth grade the writing style changes to be more expository or factual in format (Garcia & Logan, 1983). The change in writing style to the expository format often leaves students frustrated, at least if they are left on their own in figuring out how to read the text. Considering these two factors, it is important that educators be prepared to provide students with strategies for reading the various writing styles.

While the writing style is a major factor to be considered when looking at the content, the visual stimuli found in textbooks also play a major role in the presentation of information. Most educators would probably agree that textbooks containing only printed information would be boring and less than motivating for students. The stimuli in texts will usually include photographs, some in color, as well as line drawings, various types of maps, charts, and graphs. These should vary in number and complexity according to the grade, maturity, and ability levels of the intended student audience.

USE OF SOCIAL STUDIES TEXTS

As a beginning educator, most assuredly one is asked to teach a lesson from the text. The comfort of having a published program that includes a teacher's edition with detailed lesson plans and supplemental materials for teacher and student use can ease some of the nervousness often experienced by beginning educators.

While publishers provide texts as a resource for social studies instruction, it has been reported that as much as 70% to 90% of instructional time is spent with students' attention focused on information contained in the textbook alone (English, 1980; Solomon, 1976; EPIE Institute, 1976). This strategy of use of the text possibly comes about because of the comfort novice educators feel in using social studies texts as a guideline for covering specific information. Another reason some teachers follow a text carefully is because they may not feel adequately prepared to address certain topics. Rather than changing the strategy throughout the year in undertaking a study on various topics, some educators continue to follow the text without giving attention to the varied needs of students. When this practice is followed, educators are neither using the materials as the publishers intended nor are they providing an appropriate learning environment for students.

In situations where the textbook is a main component of the social studies curriculum, by focusing on student needs and interests, educators can use the content to promote learning for all. For example, if a student has difficulty in reading, the illustrations or photographs in a social studies text may be used as a foundation for instruction. Supplemental materials such as films or videos may be used as a means of primary instruction for students who are overwhelmed with the complexity of the text. Yet, for a large number of students, the textbook as a whole provides a basis for general information in a variety of areas.

As a teacher gains experience, a certain teaching style will usually emerge. The use of the textbook as an instructional tool will also be developed. This is important in the intended use of the content of the materials. With this in mind it is vital that we all, as educators, understand that no one method or use of content texts is best. Equally important is the understanding that no one book can meet all of the learning needs of the students in a given class (Fig. 2-1). Instructional decisions must be made by the teacher.

FIGURE 2-1 Interest Inventory for Social Studies (Upper Elementary and Middle School Levels)

Directions: Answer each of the questions below. This is not a test, it is a way for you to let me know what you are interested in or what you know about certain information.

1. What is your favorite holiday?

2. George Washington and Abraham Lincoln were two famous presidents. How many other presidents can you name?

3. Name one thing you would like to learn about the history of ___(your state)___ .

4. Name your favorite:
   a. book about anyone in history (fiction or nonfiction).
   b. movie about any person, place, or thing in history.

5. Do you ever watch the evening newscast?

6. Do you ever read the newspaper? If so, which sections?

7. Have you ever used a road map? Mall map? Time-zone map? Political map? Weather map?

8. What is "hemisphere"?

   In which hemisphere is our country located?

9. Do you like to travel?

   If so, what places have you visited (cities, states, countries, etc.)?

10. What kinds of activities would you like to complete in social studies this year?

EVALUATION OF SOCIAL STUDIES TEXTS

Evaluation of any materials used in an instructional setting should be an ongoing process. Materials should be evaluated prior to use, during instruction, and following instruction. In addition, materials should be evaluated on their appropriateness for assisting in the learning process for a particular class or individual.

As discussed before, textbook publishers provide materials as instructional resources. While improvements in textbooks have been made (Woodward, Elliott, & Nagel, 1986), it is important that materials be evaluated and instruction implemented according to the purposes intended by the publishers. Some materials are more appropriate than others for certain topics.

There are a number of areas that educators would be wise to consider when evaluating textbooks. The two areas probably most often considered are readability and accuracy. While these areas are of great significance, a more detailed evaluation of the textbook is more beneficial in order to determine its usefulness as an instructional resource in a particular situation.

Areas that may be included in a more detailed evaluation include:

1. Overall scope and sequence
2. Readability
3. Stereotypical information
4. Physical features
5. Visual stimuli

Not only is it important that educators have an awareness of the areas that may be included as a part of evaluation, but it is important that we understand the types of information to look for or questions to ask while looking at the material.

Overall scope and sequence. What skills, concepts, and generalizations are identified in the scope and sequence provided by the publisher? Are these in agreement with or may these be modified to meet the general requirements expected to be mastered by students according to local or state curriculum guidelines?

What is the general organization of the overall series? Is there a clear relationship between the information covered by the various grade level texts? Is there a balance in the types of information (i.e., skills, concepts, generalizations) provided? Is the balance appropriate for the level of students (i.e., elementary vs. middle school—lower to higher level)?

FIGURE 2-2 Fry Readability Graph

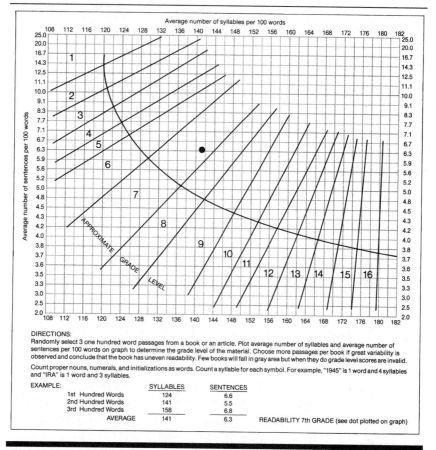

DIRECTIONS:

Randomly select 3 one hundred word passages from a book or an article. Plot average number of syllables and average number of sentences per 100 words on graph to determine the grade level of the material. Choose more passages per book if great variability is observed and conclude that the book has uneven readability. Few books will fall in gray area but when they do grade level scores are invalid.

Count proper nouns, numerals, and initializations as words. Count a syllable for each symbol. For example, "1945" is 1 word and 4 syllables and "IRA" is 1 word and 3 syllables.

EXAMPLE:	SYLLABLES	SENTENCES	
1st Hundred Words	124	6.6	
2nd Hundred Words	141	5.5	
3rd Hundred Words	158	6.8	
AVERAGE	141	6.3	READABILITY 7th GRADE (see dot plotted on graph)

SOURCE: Edward Fry, "A Readability Formula That Saves Time," Journal of Reading (April 1968), 11:587.

Readability.   While it is understood that a consistent degree of difficulty can be a problem for any content text, it is important that content be evaluated for readability overall and within chapters. This may be accomplished by using readability formulas, checklists, content reading inventory, or cloze procedures.

Stereotypical information.   Although in recent revisions textbook publishers have made great strides to improve the representation of various groups (e.g., cultural, ethnic, disabled), it is important when evaluating textbooks that this area is looked at in depth. While some checklists may

FIGURE 2-3 Textbook Readability Checklist

Using the following evaluations, rate the statements below:

      5 = Excellent
      4 = Good
      3 = Adequate
      2 = Poor
      1 = Unacceptable
    NA = Not applicable

Textbook title: _____

Publisher: _____

Copyright date: _____

_____ 1. Assumptions about students' vocabulary knowledge are appropriate.

_____ 2. Assumptions about students' prior knowledge in social studies are appropriate.

_____ 3. The teacher's manual provides the teacher with ways to develop concepts based on students' background.

_____ 4. The text introduces abstract concepts by accompanying them with concrete examples.

_____ 5. The level of sentence complexity is appropriate for the students.

_____ 6. The text avoids irrelevant details.

_____ 7. The text has a clear and simple organizational structure.

_____ 8. Questions and activities are correlated with organization of material in the text.

_____ 9. The text provides opportunities for independent practice by students.

_____ 10. The text provides graphic aids to reinforce information.

_____ 11. The text provides suggestions for activities to reinforce student learning.

_____ 12. The questions in the text are written at a variety of levels.

_____ 13. Discussion questions which encourage critical thinking are provided.

_____ 14. Unit, chapter, and subtitles are interesting and inviting.

_____ 15. The cover, format, print size, and pictures are appealing to the students.

Readability Analysis
1. Number of items on which the book was rated the lowest.
2. Areas in which these items were located:
     Organization
     Reinforcement
     Motivation
3. Number of items on which the book was rated the highest.
4. Areas in which these items were located:
     Organization
     Reinforcement
     Motivation
5. Summary of the analysis.

provide an overview, a number of checklists are available for use in evaluating the bias in materials. In evaluating materials concerning stereotypes, not only should the printed materials be observed, but photographs and drawings should also be examined for representation.

Physical features.   The textbook and accompanying materials should be
examined carefully with students in mind. For example, the type and size
of print should vary depending on the grade level, with larger print for
younger students and smaller print being used only for upper elementary
and middle school levels.

Are the materials colorful and inviting? Are the materials sturdy? Will
they last until the next adoption year? Will the supplementary materials
last? Is there a way provided to store materials (e.g., binder, box)?

Visual stimuli.   The visual stimuli included in textbooks have improved
over the years. More colorful and accurate pictures have become more
prevalent in elementary texts. In addition, the captions under the pictures,
maps, drawings, and charts are more appropriate on a grade level basis.
In evaluating materials, one might ask about the number of pictures,
maps, drawings, and charts included.

FIGURE 2-4 Content Reading Inventory

The informal reading inventory is most useful for content teachers because it can be
constructed from their textbook, or a textbook they are evaluating. The directions for
development of an inventory follows.

1. Have a particular class in mind when you develop an informal reading inventory. If you are teaching now, or know what grade level you will be teaching, aim
   your inventory for that grade.
2. Select the material to use as a basis for your informal reading inventory. It is
   better to use materials with which the students are not extremely familiar.
3. Choose at least six passages from the beginning through the end of the book:
   passages for silent reading, oral reading, and listening comprehension. The
   length of the passages will vary according to the grade level. The amount of
   time spent reading should be typical—approximately the same as the students'
   attention span. When you have chosen the passages, make copies so that you
   can mark the students' responses.
4. Develop comprehension questions for each passage. These should be based
   on the skills you expect your students to have and what you need to know
   about their ability in order to plan effectively, using a particular book. Points are
   given for answering the questions correctly.
5. If possible, give your inventory to one student prior to using with a group in
   order to become more familiar with the materials and to develop a system for
   marking errors.

FIGURE 2-5 The Cloze Procedure

The cloze procedure was developed primarily as a measure of readability to test the difficulty of instructional materials and to evaluate their appropriateness for students. While there are a number of variations on the use of the cloze, in order for it to be useful as a readability measure, certain steps must be followed.

1. Choose passages from the textbook that have differing levels of difficulty. Each passage should begin at the normal beginning of a paragraph and be at least 250 words in length. Every fifth word should be deleted, with the test having 50 deletions. Shorter passages or variation in the number of words deleted will not produce reliable results.
2. Duplicate the tests and distribute them to a class of 25 to 30 students. Students should not have read the material from which the tests were made. No time limit should be placed on completion of the test.
3. Tell the students to write on each blank the word they think was deleted. Responses are scored correct when they are an exact match, but minor misspellings should be disregarded. (In order to avoid confusion, all blanks should be the same length.)

The scoring procedure for the cloze is:

$$\frac{\text{Number of correct insertions}}{\text{number of blanks}} \times 100\%$$

Reading levels scale for traditional cloze procedure:

Independent level	58% and above
Instructional level	44% through 57%
Frustration level	43% and below

Checklist for Social Studies Texbook Evaluation

AREAS FOR EVALUATION:	RATING			
	Poor	Fair	Good	Excellent
1. Visual stimuli **a.** Pictures Color Black and white **b.** Line drawings **c.** Charts				

(Checklist continues)

Checklist for Social Studies Texbook Evaluation—cont'd

AREAS FOR EVALUATION:	RATING			
	Poor	Fair	Good	Excellent
d. Graphs **e.** Maps Color Black and white				
2. Context **a.** Vocabulary (appropriate for grade level) **b.** Sentence length **c.** Paragraph structure (appropriate for grade level)				
3. Cultural Aspects **a.** No group is stereotyped **b.** Every group is treated respectfully **c.** Males and females are treated equally				
4. Physical Features **a.** Print Readable Appropriate size Appropriate spacing between words/ paragraphs **b.** Cover Sturdy Inviting **c.** Objectives Match those of local and state guidelines **d.** Index, glossary, bibliography				

Checklist for Social Studies Texbook Evaluation—cont'd

AREAS FOR EVALUATION:	RATING			
	Poor	Fair	Good	Excellent

5. Content
   a. Information is related to Social Studies topics (state and local guidelines)
   b. Concepts and generalizations are appropriate for grade level
   c. Content is presented sequentially in the grade levels				

Also, in looking at the maps, charts, and graphs included in the textbook, it is important to question not only the usefulness but the size and use of color or shades. While these are beneficial in aiding comprehension of information, too many or those with inappropriate detail (complexity) may be an area for concern.

TEXTBOOK WORKBOOKS, WORKSHEETS, AND SUPPLEMENTARY MATERIALS

Earlier in this section, there was discussion of the various materials available to educators for reinforcement of learning experiences for students. Among these materials, in most published programs, one will find workbooks designed to accompany the textbook as well as duplicating or copy masters.

As educators it is important to consider when and how to use these materials. One consideration that must be recognized in using workbooks and worksheets is the variation in learning styles most common in your classroom. If a large portion of your students tend to be visually oriented, then printed materials would probably be useful. On the other hand, it is very important that hands-on activities be provided for those students who are more tactile in how they learn.

As a precaution for novice educators, as well as a reminder to those of us who have been in the classroom for a number of years, it is very important that we remember the intended purpose of the workbooks and worksheets as reinforcement and independent practice, not as busy work.

For example, a friend of mine who has a son in fifth grade at a local school volunteers two mornings each week to help the teacher with various projects. Her mornings for the first six weeks of the school year were spent copying each page of the resource book. Needless to say, she is less than thrilled with the implementation of the materials, that being a packet (i.e., several worksheets stapled together) being given to her son each week for completion. (Just for the record, she is currently an education major and is extremely concerned about this practice.)

This same precaution must be taken when filmstrips, videos, or computer programs are provided by publishing companies as a part of the adopted series, or purchased separately by the school. While these are meant to be used to help motivate or encourage students in the learning process through clarification, further information, or additional practice, these materials have, at times, been used as a means of keeping students entertained while the teacher did something else (e.g., graded papers, filled out report cards or progress reports, prepared lesson plans).

In summary, it is important for us to go back to the statement mentioned on several occasions. That is, the individual teacher in a particular classroom has to use his own professional judgement in deciding on the best application of lessons for the students in his class.

HELPFUL HINTS FOR UNIT 2:

1. In looking back at your school experiences, what do you remember about the social studies texts?
2. Using the evaluation checklist, evaluate a social studies program. Be prepared to compare your evaluation with those of your classmates.
3. Readability is a concern in using any content text. Using the readability formula described in this section, or one of those referred to, establish the readability for a social studies textbook at a selected grade level. You might also compare the readability levels of texts designed for elementary levels and middle school levels.
4. Define stereotype. Explain strategies you might use to recognize stereotypical information in textbooks.

REFERENCES

English, R. (1980). The politics of textbook adoption. *Phi Delta Kappan, 62,* 275–278.

EPIE Institute. (1976). *National study on the nature and quality of instructional materials used by teachers and learners.* (Report No. 76). New York: EPIE Institute Teachers College, Columbia University.

Garcia, J. and Logan J. (1983). Teaching social studies using basal readers. *Social Education, 47,* 533–535.

Hooper, J. H. and Smith, B. A. (1993). Children's U.S. history textbooks: 1787–1865. *Social Education, 57,* 18.

Solomon, M. (1978). Textbook selection committees: What teachers can do. *Learning, 6,* 43.

Woodward, A., Elliot, D. L., & Nagel, K. C. (1986). Beyond textbooks in elementary social studies. *Social Education, 50,* 50.

STUDY QUESTIONS FOR UNIT 3: 1. What three main sources often provide the basis for social studies instruction? **2.** How might reading words and reading maps and globes be similar? **3.** When should basic map reading skills be introduced? **4.** Why might activities be the ideal teaching tool for instruction in map and globe reading skills? **5.** Why is it important for individual teachers to decide when and how to use activities related to map and globe skills?

INTRODUCTION Social studies is a broad area of study. For teachers in the elementary and middle school levels, the textbook adopted for use, state and local cur-

Map and Globe Skills

riculum guides, and requirements for standardized skills assessment often become the basis for the entire focus of information covered. The purpose of this section is to discuss eight components of map and globe skills with emphasis on the need for student understanding. The eight components are direction, location, symbols, scale, community, region, nation, and world. The need for sequential development of skills is emphasized. In addition, activities that may be implemented to engage students in development of understanding of map and globe skills are described.

Maps and globes have traditionally been considered as essentials or fundamentals of social studies instruction. We, as educators, need to realize and remember that while map reading may appear simple, it requires the ability to process information abstractly. Difficulty with this is something we often share with our students. For example, how many of us have ever used the mall map while out shopping? Or had the experience of renting a vehicle in a strange city only to find ourselves overwhelmed with following the map to get out of the airport complex itself? For those fortunate few who have never felt any frustration in attempting to make sense of a map, you have the admiration, awe, and possibly the envy of the rest of us.

Being able to comprehend the information presented on maps and globes requires specialized skills and knowledge. Map reading demands decoding skills somewhat similar to those needed in order to comprehend information written in narrative form. The symbols and rules for making sense of the symbols are different, but the process of using symbols to make sense is similar. For example, students learn that certain letters make up certain words and that those words represent certain objects or concepts. On maps, certain symbols, such as dots, stars, and squares represent places or objects. Given this premise, one reason students may have difficulty with map reading is that they don't understand the form and furthermore, may not understand what the information on the map represents.

Given this information, the question of when map and globe skills should be introduced and in what order they should be introduced must be addressed. Sources of information regarding the exact skills needed by students at the elementary level are inconsistent. In looking at a number of textbook series, various programs require different skills for students. (See Unit Two for further discussion of textbooks.)

A number of groups have provided suggested scope and sequence for teaching map and globe skills. In Table 3-1, the sample scope and sequence developed by the Joint Committee on Geographic Education of the National Council on Geographic Education and the Association of American Geographers (1984) is presented.

Because all students do not enter the formal school setting with the same prior experiences related to maps and globes, it is important that teachers be aware of the need for presentation of skills in a sequential manner, yet at the levels of need identified for the particular students with whom she may be working. Introduction of basic skills should be included at the kindergarten level with more specific skills being introduced as the students reach higher maturaty, ability, and experiential levels.

TABLE 3-1 Map and Globe Skills: Suggested Scope and Sequence

Grade Level	Skills
Kindergarten	1. Knows and uses terms related to location, direction, and distance 2. Recognizes a globe as a model of the earth 3. Recognizes and uses terms that express relative size and shape 4. Identifies school and local community by name 5. Recognizes and uses models and symbols to represent real things
Grade One	1. Knows geographic location of home in relation to school and neighborhood 2. Knows the layout of the school campus 3. Uses simple classroom maps to locate objects 4. Identifies state and nation by name 5. Follows and gives verbal directions 6. Distinguishes between land and water symbols on globes and maps 7. Relates locations on maps and globes to locations on earth 8. Observes, describes, and builds simple models and maps of the local environment
Grade Two	1. Makes and uses simple maps of school and home neighborhoods 2. Interprets map symbols using a legend 3. Knows and uses cardinal directions 4. Locates one's community, state, and nation on maps and globes 5. Identifies local landforms 6. Differentiates between maps and globes 7. Locates other neighborhoods on maps 8. Traces routes within and between neighborhoods using a variety of maps and models 9. Compares pictures and maps of the same area
Grade Three	1. Uses distance, direction, scale, and map symbols 2. Compares own community with other communities 3. Compares urban and rural environments
Grade Four	1. Interprets pictures, graphs, charts, and tables 2. Works with distance, direction, scale, and map symbols 3. Relates similarities and differences between maps and globes 4. Uses maps of different scales and themes 5. Recognizes the common characteristics of map grid systems 6. Compares and contrasts regions on a state, national, or world basis
Grade Five	1. Recognizes distance, direction, scale, map symbols, and the relationship of maps and globes 2. Works with longitude and latitude 3. Uses maps, charts, graphs, and tables to display data 4. Discusses location in terms of where and why

(table continues)

TABLE 3-1 Map and Globe Skills: Suggested Scope and Sequence—cont'd

Grade Level	Skills
Grade Five— cont'd	5. Maps the correspondence between resources and industry 6. Maps physical and cultural regions in North America
Grade Six	1. Improves understanding of location, relative location, and the importance of location 2. Uses maps, globes, charts, and graphs 3. Readily uses latitude, longitude, map symbols, time zones, and basic earth-sun relationships 4. Gains insight about the interaction of climate, landforms, natural vegetation, and other interactions in physical regions 5. Maps trade routes, particularly those connecting developed and developing nations 6. Plots distributions of population and key resources on regional maps

It is important for teachers to remember that each skill related to reading maps and globes can be understood at many levels of sophistication. In well-planned programs, the skills are developed as students progress through the traditional grade levels. The most important factor that must be remembered in helping students develop understanding is to present information realistically, being careful not to overestimate students' abilities to work effectively with maps and globes. Active student involvement in activities that require use of specific skills is one suggestion teachers may implement in order to help students become successful in working with maps and globes.

On the following pages, discussion about each of the eight identified areas will be provided. In addition, activities that emphasize basic skills at a variety of levels will be presented. Some activities may be more appropriate for lower levels; however, teachers are encouraged to try activities that they feel might be needed by their particular students disregarding the suggested levels.

COMMUNITY

If you call to order pizza, one of the questions usually asked concerns not only your address but information about the specific section of town in which you live. Where we currently live, the area we always name is Cedar Knoll, but our home is actually a couple of blocks away. In our community we have a number of single family dwellings and one block of condominiums. While growing up, I lived in a little rural community called Pumpkin Center. There we had scattered houses and little farms the length of a road five miles long.

The definition or concept of community is not static. For one group of students one definition may be appropriate, while it may be difficult or almost incomprehensible for others. At one grade level, a community may be considered the center of a student's surroundings, where at another level, the community may mean the whole of the city.

The inclusion of community as an area of study in social studies even precedes the common use of published social studies programs. In the 1930s and 1940s, a great emphasis was placed on using the community as a grounding point for further study. In the Expanding Environments Curriculum, the focus on study of the community follows closely behind the recognition of self and family. (Barr, Barth, & Shermis, 1977).

In our society today, it is even more important that we return to a better sense of community pride and unity. In order for this to take place, not only do students need to learn about the concept of community, but students actually need to learn about their *own* community.

Our society is mobile. Because families move from one part of the country to another, it is quite common for students to be unfamiliar with the historical, cultural, or geographical makeup of their community. It is important that we, as educators, plan appropriate lessons and activities that will afford students opportunities for learning in this area.

In addition, since one of the most important aspects of social studies is development of cultural understanding on a global basis, we must provide students with opportunities to learn about the similarities and differences in community structure from various parts of the United States and the world. While textbook publishers provide some basic information about various types of communities, it is up to the individual educator to decide on the needs of the students he works with as well as the additional activities that may be needed.

ACTIVITIES

ACTIVITIES RELATED TO COMMUNITY
Our School

Time Allotment: One class period, as needed

Materials: Colored masking tape, transparency of floor plan of school, yarn or string, copies of floor plan for students

Grade Level: Lower elementary

Our School **continued**

Procedure: Arrows for walking are taped to floor. Have the students walk the arrows, then study arrows drawn on floor plan map. Students can measure distances with yarn or string and compare to see which is longer or shorter. Alternative activity: Have the students label a floor plan of the school while sitting in the classroom. Exchange maps and check for accuracy.

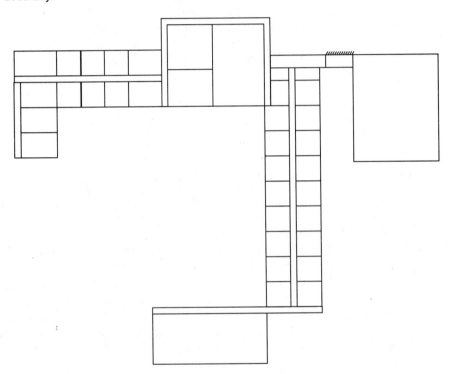

Our School and Neighborhood

Time Allotment: Four or five class periods

Materials: Large paper, little blocks or pieces of cardboard or colored paper

Grade Level: Elementary and middle school

Procedure: Take a walk around the school and neighboring area, having students take notes or make sketches of what they see. Separate the class into groups and give each group a large piece of paper to be used as a map. Students place school (using blocks or cardboard) on the map, and then draw in or use colored paper for the school grounds, surrounding streets, buildings, adjacent area (pool, woods). If students cannot remember or

Our School and Neighborhood **continued**

disagree, repeat the walk. Continue until the map is complete. Alternative activity: This same activity could be done for a neighborhood shopping area.

Planning a New Community

Time Allotment: Two or three class periods

Materials: Art supplies, boxes, butcher paper

Grade Level: Elementary and middle school

Procedure: Cover large tables with paper. Students decide what the community needs and use milk cartons, boxes, etc. to lay out what they believe makes up a good community. Then each student makes a map of the new community, including a legend that symbolizes land forms, buildings, parks, shopping center, etc.

Alternative activity: Invite a city planner to speak to the class. Following this visit, the students may complete the activity in groups rather than individually, depending on the complexity decided on for their guidelines.

Tracing Our Community

Time Allotment: Three or four class periods

Materials: Transparency that shows the streets, buildings, and major land forms around the school and immediate neighborhood, butcher paper, markers

Grade Level: Elementary

Procedure: Project transparency from projector onto a large piece of butcher paper. Have the students trace in streets, land forms, buildings. Then each student should locate her own home and label it. Have the students locate and label stores, schools, and other buildings familiar to them.

Let Your Fingers Do the Walking

Time Allotment: One or two class periods

Materials: Map of community, telephone book yellow pages (several copies), paper, pencils, chalkboard or transparency

Grade Level: Elementary and middle school

Procedure: Talk with students about the importance of the yellow pages as being a place where businesses and professionals can provide information for interested people. For example, have the students look up the "physicians" section and talk about its importance. You may also discuss how to look up several types of businesses as examples.

Let Your Fingers Do the Walking **continued**

Have the students look up a number of items (see suggested list). They will want to make reference to the community map in order to find the best answer.

List the name, address, and phone number for:

1. The nearest place to buy goldfish.
2. The nearest foreign car dealer.
3. A place to buy hay for your horses.
4. A nearby place to have a prescription filled.
5. A dishwasher repairer.
6. A place to have film developed.
7. The nearest electrician.
8. A place to rent videos.
9. The nearest skating rink, arcade, or bowling alley.
10. A place where you can order a pizza.

The Homes in Our Community

Time Allotment: One or two class periods

Materials: Markers, butcher paper, drawing paper, pictures from the community (if possible)

Grade Level: Elementary

Procedure: With the students' help, prepare a list of all the different kinds of structures people in your community call home. Create as long a list as possible. From the list, select types of homes to be used in a graphing activity. Select the types of homes that are most familiar to your students; these might include single-family dwellings, mobile homes, duplexes, apartments, condominiums, or town houses.

On the board, make a graph (see example). Then ask each student to tell in which type of

The Homes In Our Community

mobile home	⌂ ⌂ ⌂ ⌂ ⌂
condominium	⌂ ⌂ ⌂
apartment	⌂ ⌂ ⌂ ⌂
house	⌂ ⌂ ⌂ ⌂ ⌂ ⌂ ⌂
town house	⌂ ⌂
duplex	⌂

The Homes in Our Community **continued**

home they live. As each student responds, draw a symbol on the graph. It should be made clear to the students that each symbol represents one home.

After the entire class has had an opportunity to respond, help students draw conclusions about the information. How many students live in each type of home? Which type of home do we think we have the most of in our community, based on our graph? The least amount?

Variation: Use the pictures of various types of homes found in the community as a beginning point for the above activity. Students may also draw the type of home they live in. Using the community map drawn in a previous activity, students may locate the parts of the community in which various types of homes may be located.

This Is Your Community

Time Allotment: One or two class periods

Materials: Photographs of industrial and public buildings in the area, map of community, guest speaker, bulletin board

Grade Level: Elementary and middle school

Procedure: Locate and collect photographs of industrial and public buildings in the area. Introduce the buildings to students by discussing what goes on inside. Have the students locate the buildings on the community map. Have the students write about the various buildings and post this information along with the photographs on a bulletin board entitled "This Is Your Community." Variation: Take a field trip to some of the industrial or public buildings. Students should note terrain in addition to the surrounding structures. Another variation would be to invite guest speakers to discuss what goes on inside the various buildings.

Getting To Know the Post Office

Time Allotment: One or two class periods

Materials: Addresses of friends or relatives (should be supplied by students), map of community showing various zip codes, field trip to the post office or guest speaker

Grade Level: Elementary and middle school

Procedure: In order to familiarize students with the purpose and daily operation of the post office (beyond that explored at the primary and lower elementary levels), discuss or invite a guest speaker to describe the daily operation of the post office. If at all possible, focus should be given to the importance of correct addresses, with emphasis on the zip code. A map of the community showing the various zip code zones should be available for the students' use. Using their prepared list of addresses, students should identify the various parts of the community in which their friends or relatives live, based on the zip code map. Variation: A field trip to the post office in which the students have the opportunity to see the various methods used for sorting mail would be especially helpful in providing a valuable experience for students.

continued

Life Back Then

Time Allotment: Two or three class periods

Materials: Senior citizen interview forms, maps of community from various dates (e.g., ten years ago, twenty years ago), photographs of the community at various points in history, butcher paper or chalkboard, pens or chalk

Grade Level: Elementary and middle school

Procedure: Give students a copy of a senior citizen interview form (see example) and ask them to have it completed by a certain date. Discuss with the class the importance of learning about the background of the community in order to understand the reasons certain changes have taken place. On a bulletin board, post maps of the community from various dates along with photographs depicting the community at various points in history.

After students have completed the interviews, compare the findings of the students. Locate various places metnioned by the senior citizens on the maps. Discuss how the community has changed in terms of size.

Variation: Invite a senior citizen to the class to discuss the history of the community and the changes he has seen. Students should be prepared with appropriate questions.

SENIOR CITIZEN INTERVIEW

The interview should be brief and informal. It is important that you state the purpose of the interview at the beginning. You may find that the senior citizen you talk with will want to add information about her personal life as well as a discussion of topics studied in school. Please be patient and try to gain as much information as possible.

Below is a list of questions you may use to help guide the interview. Please do not limit yourself to these questions.

1. How long have you lived in this community?
2. What kinds of businesses were here when you were about my age?
3. Did you go to school here (elementary, middle, secondary)?
4. What was your first job? Where was the business located?
5. What were the homes like in our community at your earliest recollection or when you moved here? If you haven't lived here very long, maybe you can tell me how where you used to live compares to where we live now?

The interviewer should close the interview and thank the senior citizen. Please write up a summary of the information you learned during the interview. Please be sure your handwriting is neat, and write only on the front of the paper.

continued

Likenesses and Differences

Time Allotment: Varied

Materials: Addresses for pen pals, letter-writing materials (paper, pencils, envelopes, stamps), pictures of your community, pictures of your school

Grade Level: Elementary and middle school

Procedure: After securing the addresses for pen pals for each student from another school and at about the same grade level, ask the class to write individual pen pals. In the letter, not only should personal information be included (e.g., age, interests, description of self) but also a description of the school. These letters, along with pictures of the school should be sent to the pen pals. After receiving a similar response from the pen pals, students should again write concerning the community. These letters may be accompanied by student-drawn maps of the community and pictures of the community. The process should be continued throughout the school year and emphasis should be placed on the similarities and differences between the two communities. Note: If at all possible, allow the students to take pictures themselves, using a simple "point and shoot" or Polaroid camera. Variation: Have the students tape a class video in addition to the letters. A video about the school and community may also be made.

Pen pal addresses may be obtained from:

Student Letter Exchange   League of Friendship, Inc.
630 Third Avenue   P.O. Box 509
New York, NY 10017   Mount Vernon, OH 43050

REGION

When we hear the term region, most of us think of the region of the United States where we currently live. The second thought that comes to mind is probably the result of studying geography—either at the elementary or middle school level—where we learned about desert regions, tropical regions, or frigid regions of the world.

Given this background, when we attempt to teach about regions, we as educators and facilitators of learning would probably be wise to think carefully about our students and what they need to know about the concept. For students at the lower elementary levels, region may be defined in terms of physical space. For example, the space in the classroom where the social studies center is located may be one region while the science center is in another region of the classroom. This information may be used as a basis of understanding that regions are located in various spaces (or places) and usually have characteristics that make them different from one another. In terms of mapping experiences at the lower elementary level, three-dimensional maps of the classroom may be made to reinforce understanding. These of course can be expanded on as the students develop understanding.

As cognitive growth takes place, the definition increases to include more abstract boundaries and to be able to take part in activities to reinforce the understanding of regions in terms of geography, history, and culture within the context of the United States as well as a more global view.

ACTIVITIES

ACTIVITIES RELATED TO REGION
What Is A Characteristic?

Time Allotment: One or two class periods

Materials: Sheets with characteristics listed, transparency with examples, pencils

Grade Level: Upper elementary and middle school

Procedure: Following a discussion about characteristics, have the students complete a worksheet similar to the example. Follow this with a discussion of the various definitions or criteria used for the choices made by students.

This may be used as an introduction to a lesson about various regions of the United States or the world, based on the fact that the term regions can be defined as places that share common characteristics.

PEOPLE AND THEIR CHARACTERISTICS

What is a characteristic? _____

_____

Here are some characteristics. Can you think of people who fit these descriptions? Circle those you can and write out the name of the person it made you think of in the space provided. (REMEMBER: you will have to provide your reason, and you will have to share out loud!)

brave	_____	honest	_____
serious	_____	friendly	_____
demanding	_____	gentle	_____

continues

What Is A Characteristic? **continued**

funny	_____	adventurous	_____
messy	_____	neat	_____
sad	_____	joyful	_____
short	_____	tall	_____
cooperative	_____	dainty	_____
lovable	_____	prim	_____
pretty	_____	fun-loving	_____
popular	_____	quiet	_____
self-confident	_____	lazy	_____
happy	_____	witty	_____
smart	_____	tireless	_____

Add some of your own:

_____   _____

_____   _____

Boundaries

Time Allotment: Two or three class periods

Materials: Butcher paper, markers, playground

Grade Level: Elementary and middle school

Procedure: A region does not necessarily have to be a vast area of territory; it can be quite limited. Students should develop a map of the school playground. After the map is drawn, boundaries for the various regions may be drawn in. Examples of regions might include:

baseball-playing region   soccer region
swings region   see-saw region

Boundaries **continued**

no running region	space for running region
merry-go-round region	slide region
water fountain region	walkway to school region

The list should be adapted to fit the particular school and age group of students. Also, the complexity of the map should be based on the age and experience level of the students.

As a follow up, discussion can lead the students to a better understanding of the permanence of regions or how they may change over time. This would lead to a discussion of other types of boundaries and what they mean.

Four Corners of the Country

Time Allotment: One or two class periods

Materials: Duplicated copies of a U.S. map (see example), four different colored markers for each student, large U.S. map

Grade Level: Elementary

Procedure: After an introductory lesson on regions, students may have questions regarding the region of the country in which they live. While there are many different views on the methods for dividing the United States into regions, one simple way is to divide the continental United States into four parts. While showing the students a large U.S. map, show how there are basically four different areas—Northeast, Southeast, Southwest, and Northwest. The students may color the map showing the four different areas. It is also very important that you explain that Alaska and Hawaii are not included in the four regions being discussed as a part of this activity. Variation: Since the activity is relatively low level, you may have the students simply fold a duplicated map of the United States to give them the idea of the four regions. You may also have the students label their home state or the states in the region nearest where they live.

Where On the World Are We

Time Allotment: One or two class periods

Materials: Duplicated copies of a blank globe, markers, crayons, large drawing of blank globe on chart paper (or transparency)

Grade Level: Elementary and middle school

Where On the World Are We **continued**

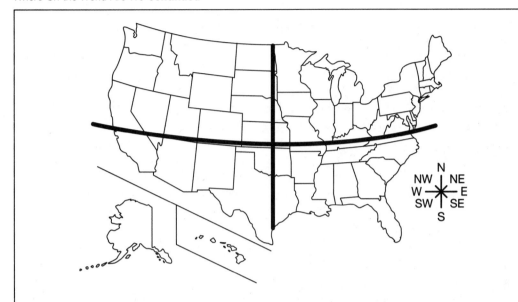

Procedure: After a study of the three major global regions (i.e., polar regions, temperate regions, and tropical regions), as a class, label and describe each of the regions on the globe. Have the students identify the region in which they live. You may have the students use certain colors for each of the regions. Variation: You may use the same general map to discuss the concept of lattitude and hemisphere.

The Three Major Global Regions

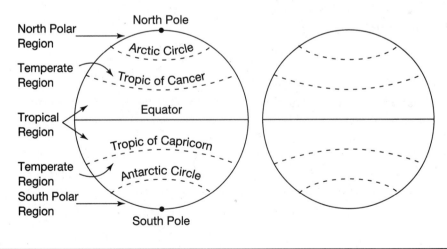

continued

Using A Weather Map

Time Allotment: One or two class periods

Materials: Weather maps and information from newspapers, map showing regions of the continental United States

Grade Level: Upper elementary and middle school

Procedure: Have the students bring in the weather maps from various newspapers (some newspapers carry colored maps in the Sunday edition). Talk about the way the weather varies depending on the area or region of the country in which you live. Have the students find the approximate location of their community region and note between which temperature lines it falls. Locate other similar regions and compare the temperatures. Students may enjoy listening to a weather broadcast from the National Weather Service. This is broadcast continuously on VHF-FM at 162.40 and 162.55 MHz.

Desert Regions

Time Allotment: One or two class periods

Materials: Large maps or maps in social studies texts showing desert regions of the globe, globe, sand paper, glue, pictures of desert regions, poster paper, construction paper (blue, green, etc.)

Grade Level: Elementary and middle school

Procedure: Use maps, globes, pictures, and charts to locate desert regions. Ask the students to define characteristics or terms that relate to desert: lack of rainfall, temperature, weathering, winds, soil, etc. Compare the deserts of the southwestern United States to desert regions in other countries. As a follow up, have the students make a desert using the sandpaper as the soil and green and blue construction paper to represent water and land. Students should make posters from their projects.

Ocean Regions

Time Allotment: One or two class periods

Materials: Large maps or maps in social studies texts showing ocean regions, globe, glue, construction paper (blue, brown, green, etc.), pictures of ocean regions, poster paper

Grade Level: Elementary and middle school

Procedure: Use maps, globes, pictures, and charts to locate ocean regions. Ask the students to define characteristics or terms that relate to ocean: currents, tides, waves, ocean floor, oceanography, etc. Compare life on the Pacific coast of the United States to that on the Atlantic coast of the United States or Europe. Students should make posters of the

Ocean Regions **continued**

various information they learn about ocean regions. Variation: To add interest, have students make wave bottles. Using clear, empty, clean soda containers (with lids), the students should fill about 1/4 full with salad or vegetable oil. Fill about 1/4 more of the container with water and blue food coloring. Place the lid on very tightly. By moving the container back and forth, the students will be able to observe a "wave."

Landforms

Time Allotment: One or two class periods

Materials: Magazines, scissors, glue, butcher paper, markers or pens, reference materials (encyclopedias, atlases, globes)

Grade Level: Elementary and middle school

Procedure: After a study of various landforms, have students find pictures in magazines that illustrate the different landforms. For example, plains, hills, deserts, plateaus, mountains, deltas.

The students should cut out pictures that illustrate the various landforms.

Divide a piece of butcher paper (48 to 60 inches long) into six columns. The students should glue the pictures under the appropriate heading. The class may be divided into groups, with each group being responsible for a landform. Each group might write a summary explaining the definition of their landform and a rationale for the inclusion of each picture being posted under the various headings.

In What Kind of Place Did It Happen?

Time Allotment: One or two class periods

Materials: Newspapers, scissors, glue, butcher paper

Grade Level: Upper elementary and middle school

Procedure: Geography, the physical aspects of a place, often plays an important part in the news (e.g., lowlands flood, avalanches happen on snow-covered mountains). Students should look through newspapers and see how many news items they can find in which geography plays a key role. The students should cut out the articles and write a brief explanation about how geographical regions played a part.

Where Is This?

Time Allotment: One or two class periods

Materials: Newspapers, magazines, scissors, glue, construction and butcher paper

Grade Level: Elementary and middle school

Where Is This? **continued**

Procedure: In newspapers or magazines find pictures of various locations. Have the students cut out the pictures and glue them onto pieces of construction paper. The students should try to identify the location or type of region that is depicted in others' pictures. These may then be displayed under regional headings on a piece of butcher paper or a bulletin board.

NATION

Not so long ago, it seemed that every tabloid show on television, as well as a large proportion of the major network news broadcasts, were filled with stories of how students labeled states and oceans incorrectly. The cry went up that the students in our schools today were receiving insufficient instruction about our nation, about where it is located from a global perspective, how it is a group of states functioning as one nation, and how because of its size and geography there are various regional characteristics.

Recently when I was visiting with a group of second graders, it was quite refreshing that they were able to tell me they lived not only in a given state but that it was a part of the nation called the United States of America. Given the background experiences of the individuals who were in the class, it was easy to see why they understood the concept. They were at a school located on a U.S. military installation; therefore, the majority of the students had lived in various places over a period of time.

For most students, the development of understanding related to nation comes about over a period of time. It is hoped that by the time students leave the primary levels of elementary school (kindergarten to grade two or three) they will have an understanding of the concept of nation. As students mature and gain experiences, it is desirable that they develop an understanding of the different nations that may be located on a given part of the globe. In our nonstatic world, they too will see the changes that take place, that is, the changes as nations emerge or are dissolved.

ACTIVITIES

ACTIVITIES RELATED TO NATION
My Nation Is

Time Allotment: One or two class periods

My Nation Is **continued**

Materials: Large map or transparency of North America, duplications for students, atlases, social studies textbooks, crayons or markers, pens, pencils

Grade Level: Elementary

Procedure: After studying the continent of North America, have students label their nation. In addition, have them label the nations that border the United States.

Variation: If students have studied about the regions found in the United States, have them draw in lines to indicate the four major regions and possibly color each differently.

My nation is _____ .

continued

We're Going on a Trip

Time Allotment: One or two class periods

Materials: Road maps (state, regional, and national), highlight pens or markers

Grade Level: Elementary and middle school

Procedure: Obtain enough road maps so that each student or small group of students can work with one. Plan a trip—a vacation of sorts—that requires the students to travel through more than one state. The students should estimate the number of miles to be traveled, the places to be seen along the way, and how long it would take to get from one place to another. This information should be summarized and posted beside the map on which they have marked their proposed route. These should be displayed on the wall or on a bulletin board.

This is Where I've Lived

Time Allotment: One or two class periods

Materials: Road maps (state, regional, and national), highlight pens or markers, yarn or string, tape

Grade Level: Elementary and middle school

Procedure: Obtain enough road maps so that each student can have an appropriate map to work with based on his background. Students should locate communities in which they have lived and highlight each one. Then students should use yarn to connect the various places. Each place should be numbered in the order the student lived there or by year.

States and Capitals

Time Allotment: Two or three class periods

Materials: Two sets of cards with the names of the state capitals, one set of cards with the names of the states

Grade Level: Upper elementary and middle school

Procedure: After a study of the states and capitals, as a culminating or reinforcement activity, use this game. Give each student a card with the name of a state capital on it. One student may be chosen to call out the names of the states, using the cards or a list. Have the class stand in a circle. As the student in the middle of the circle calls out the name of a state, the two students who have the cards with the name of the capital try to swap places. At the same time, the student in the middle tries to get into one of their places. If she succeeds, the student who does not have a place in the circle stays in the middle. This process continues until all students have had an opportunity to exchange places. Variation: Other nations and their capitals could be used.

continued

All Across the Nation

Time Allotment: Varied

Materials: U.S. wall map, maps in social studies texts, atlas, reference books, cards with names of cities or cities and states

Grade Level: Elementary and middle school

Procedure: Write the names of places in the United States on index cards. The students may prepare cards as they study various places or areas of interest. Students may get the cards to use individually at their desks or with a partner. They should try to locate the cities and states. If they have problems, they should use the index in the atlas and what they have learned about using grids to locate information.

Nations Differ in Size

Time Allotment: One or two class periods

Materials: World map, atlas, globe

Grade Level: Upper elementary and middle school

Procedure: Students should identify two or three nations on a map. A comparison of land area and water area should be made. This will help the students to understand that all nations are not the same size. Variation: Students may wish to explore other differences between nations, such as cultural, political, or economic differences.

Westward Bound

Time Allotment: Two or three class periods

Materials: Blank U.S. maps, transparencies showing the general routes taken by early expeditions and wagon trains, colored pens, reference books (encyclopedias, trade books)

Grade Level: Upper elementary and middle school

Procedure: While studying the history of the United States, it is important that students become aware of the barriers that existed and had to be overcome in order for the early pioneers to be successful. First, show the students how there were no or very few trails beyond the East Coast. Using overlays, show how the early explorers first followed routes used by the Native Americans. As this discussion takes place, students should develop their own maps. Barriers that might be included in the discussion could be deserts, mountain ranges, rivers and lakes, food shortages, and so forth. Variation: Prepare similar transparencies for those early explorers of our nation.

continued

"My" State and City

Time Allotment: Two or three class periods

Materials: Large map of the United States

Grade Level: Elementary

Procedure: Using the students' names, match them to the first letter of states and cities. For example:

Allen, Adam: Alaska, Akron
Mike, Maggie: Massachusetts, Missouri

Have the students write their names on states that have the same first letter. After students have written names on the map, discuss those states that have no student names on them. Try to think of national figures or people from the community to fill in the blank states.

We are U.S.

Time Allotment: One or two class periods

Materials: Large map of North America showing the United States, magazines, scissors, glue

Grade Level: Elementary and middle school

Procedure: Students should cut out pictures of all kinds of people from the magazines and cover the map with pictures in collage fashion. After the collage is completed, the teacher or the students should draw in the state outlines. (This may be accomplished using a transparency of the United States and an overhead projector.) The notion is to help students develop an understanding of the makeup of the society in our nation. Variation: Students should trace family backgrounds to show how families makeup the United States.

Tour Guide

Time Allotment: Two or three class periods

Materials: Magazines, scissors, glue, construction paper, pens, pencils, markers

Grade Level: Elementary and middle school

Procedure: Students should identify places of interest in the United States that they believe others would like to visit. They should cut pictures from magazines to use in travel brochures they will make to tell about the places. After gluing the pictures onto the construction paper, they should write brief descriptions about the place and why people should visit. This will encourage students to learn more about their nation and why it is interesting.

WORLD

Even for those of us who believe we are capable of thinking abstractly for a large portion of our day, the concept of "world" can be a little overwhelming. If this is the reality for us, how do we expect students at the elementary and middle school levels to understand and explain the concept of world?

In thinking about the need for an understanding of the world as a whole, it is quite clear that in order for this to be a reality, students need to have a solid understanding of the role they have as a part of a community and nation. In social studies, one way of helping students understand world is to focus on learning about the globe. While learning how to use the globe, information about various places on the globe may be explored.

ACTIVITIES

ACTIVITIES RELATED TO WORLD
Globes and Oranges

Time Allotment: One or two class periods

The World

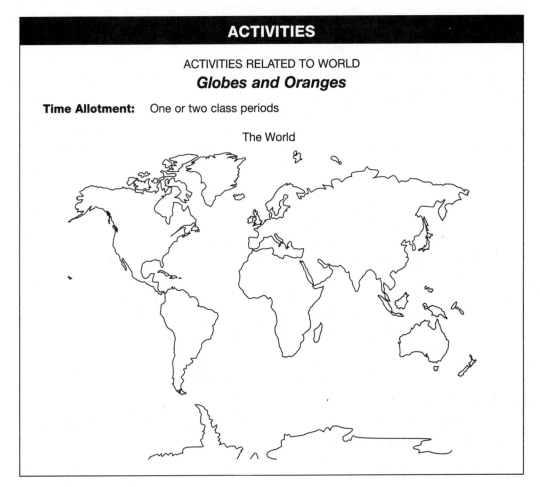

Materials: Oranges for entire class, waxed paper, plastic knives, globe, wall map of the world

Grade Level: Elementary

Procedure: Explain to the students that the earth is round like an orange; because the globe is a model of the earth, it is round, too. Maps are drawn on flat sheets of paper and do not show the earth as accurately as the globe. Whenever you show a round object on a flat piece of paper, you have a problem.

To see why mapmakers have trouble showing the round earth on a flat sheet of paper, try to flatten an orange without tearing the peel. To do so, you must make a number of cuts in the peel. Variation: When studying about the concept of hemisphere, have the students try to flatten out half of an orange.

The Continents

Time Allotment: One or two class periods

Materials: Wall map of the world, duplicated sheets

Grade Level: Elementary and middle school

Procedure: Depending on the geographer, there are either six or seven continents: North America, South America, Australia, Africa, Antarctica, Europe, and Asia (or Eurasia, which combines the latter two). Students should label the continents after identifying them on the map. Variation: A comparison of the locations of the continents.

What Constitutes a Continent?

Time Allotment: One or two class periods

Materials: World wall map, globe(s), duplicated sheets

Grade Level: Elementary and middle school

Procedure: A continent is a huge land mass (at least one million square miles) separated from other land masses usually by water, although a mountain range is a natural divide between Europe and Asia. After defining and locating the continents on the globe and map, students should label the continents. Variation: The students should label the continents by their shape and place them in order on a map.

But What About Greenland?

Time Allotment: One or two class periods

Materials: Globe(s), world map(s) (at least one wall map), encyclopedias, atlases

Grade Level: Elementary and middle school

Procedure: Often students will look at a world map and ask, "Why is Australia a continent and Greenland not?" If we look at a globe, the answer is obvious: Australia dwarfs Greenland in size, but because maps distort global representations near the poles, it appears that Greenland is larger. To alleviate this, emphasize that the globe is an accurate representation of the earth, and use the globe for learning about the continents. For reinforcement, students should look at the statistics for Greenland in comparison with Australia in reference books.

Why Is There No Arctic Continent?

Time Allotment: One class period

Materials: Globe(s), world map(s), encyclopedias, atlases

Grade Level: Elementary

Procedure: Since Antarctica is one of the continents, students sometimes ask about the Arctic. It is important that students understand that if somehow the polar caps were to melt, land would be found at the South Pole (Antarctica) and only water at the North Pole.

The LONG Lines are LONGitude

Time Allotment: One or two class periods

Materials: Globe(s), encyclopedias, reference materials

Grade Level: Upper elementary and middle school

Procedure: After an introduction of the concept of longitude, students often need a way to remember the difference between the terms longitude and latitude. One way of helping students is to reinforce that the long lines are called longitude by focusing on the word LONG.

What Are the Effects of Latitude?

Time Allotment: One or two class periods

Materials: Globe(s), encyclopedias, reference materials

Grade Level: Upper elementary and middle school

Procedure: After an introduction of the concept of latitude, students need to be able to relate the term to concrete experiences. By first locating their own area by latitude (and longitude), and talking about the various effects it has on daily life, students can then make comparisons of other areas with their own area. Effects which may be considered include: climate, precipitation, growing season, crops, lifestyle. Variation: Rather than having a whole class activity, cooperative learning strategies, such as Jigsaw, could be implemented.

continued

One Big Ocean

Time Allotment: One class period

Materials: Globe(s), world map(s), encyclopedias, atlases, reference books, duplicated sheets

Grade Level: Elementary

Procedure: The Atlantic, the Pacific, the Indian, and the Arctic oceans really make up one large ocean. They are divided into four ocean areas for convenience because of the locations of the land masses. After identifying the locations of the oceans, students should label each ocean area. The differences between the oceans should be noted and captions written accordingly.

Where Am I?

Time Allotment: One or two class periods

Materials: Globe(s), index cards, markers

Grade Level: Upper elementary and middle school

Procedure: Students should write a description of a place on their index card, such as:

I am a country south of the equator.
My latitude is _____ degrees.
My longitude is _____ degrees.

They will need to use a globe to help write the description. After all the descriptions are written, the cards should be collected and the students will try to guess the various countries based on the descriptions.

It's a Small World

Time Allotment: One or two class periods

Materials: Globe(s), world map(s)

Grade Level: Elementary

Procedure: Involve the students in a class discussion about what international contacts members of students' families have had recently. Examples might be: travel to another country, a letter from someone overseas, a meeting with someone from another part of the world (even if through technological advances such as satellite hook-ups). The various countries should be located and labeled on the globe or world map.

continued

Half A Globe

Time Allotment: One or two class periods

Materials: Globe(s), world map(s), reference materials, duplicated sheets, oranges or styrofoam balls

Grade Level: Elementary and middle school

Procedure: Students may have some difficulty understanding the term hemisphere. Explain to students that they should think of the earth as a ball or sphere. The equator is an imaginary line going east and west around the largest part of the earth; that line divides the earth into two halves. The prime meridian is an imaginary line that goes between the North and South Poles. These two imaginary lines can cut the earth into halves (*hemi* means half). Students should decide which hemisphere they want to show, Northern or Southern, Eastern or Western, and cut their oranges or styrofoam balls accordingly.

DIRECTION

If you ever have the opportunity to talk with a group of adults about visiting an unfamiliar place, you will find that without doubt one of the most frustrating experiences is getting lost. At its most primary level, direction can be defined as up or down, right or left. In a more complex definition, direction may deal with north, south, east, west, and various related terms.

Test Your Students' Directional Sense

Give the following test to your class before you teach about directions. Afterward, give the test again. Then compare the two test results. You and your students will probably be pleased with the improvements made in understanding.

Directions: Put an X in front of each correct answer.

1.   I am going toward the east and turn left into a street. I am now going toward what direction?

_____   north

_____   east

_____ south

_____ west

2. I am lying in bed on my stomach with my head toward the south. Which wall of the room is to my left?

    _____   north wall

    _____   south wall

    _____   east wall

    _____   west wall

3. A boy stands on a beach and looks out toward the sunset. Then he turns to the right. In which direction has he turned?

    _____   north

    _____   south

    _____   east

    _____   west

4. When I get up each morning, the sun shines through my bedroom window on a closet in the middle of the opposite wall. When I stand in the middle of the room facing the door, the closet is to my right. In which wall is the door?

    _____   north wall

    _____   south wall

    _____   east wall

    _____   west wall

Answer key: 1. north, 2. east wall, 3. north, 4. south wall

> For students, and for all of us, learning to read, follow, and give information regarding direction is important. While we often take this ability for granted, it involves the understanding of a number of basic skills. Among these are the ability to read grid lines, orient maps correctly, and follow a compass.

TABLE 3-2 How to Offset the Notion That North Is Up and South Is Down

1. Post azimuthal projections of the earth in which "up north" and "down south" do not apply. Most modern atlases have at least one such projection.
2. Occasionally invert maps and globes, pointing out that their position does not make them wrong.
3. Plan a drill in which students point to a river on a wall map. Then make such statements as "the Po flows down and east."
4. Plan a drill in which students point sequentially to the cardinal directions, naming each; then have them point up and down.

While labeling the walls of the classroom is widely accepted as a way of emphasizing direction, it is very important that the walls be labeled correctly; that is, North really facing North, South is South, and so on. This can be extended to labeling the playground boundaries, lunchrooms, and resource room or library. By having walls labeled, it is easier for students to learn that just because the wall at the front of their classroom faces North, the front wall in the library may face another direction.

In order to help students develop understanding, they need to be provided with ample opportunities for hands-on experiences and activities dealing with direction. This is sometimes an area that teachers feel a little uncomfortable about unless they too have had the opportunity to have experiences with direction. One of the activities I always use with students is to have them explore or go on a scavenger hunt of sorts following directions (e.g., go down the north stairs, walk out the door, turn south) and using a simple compass.

ACTIVITIES

ACTIVITIES RELATED TO DIRECTION
These Are the Places in Our Neighborhood

Time Allotment: One or two class periods

Materials: Simple compass for each pair of students, permission for leaving school campus

Grade Level: Upper elementary and middle school

Procedure: Plan a walking field trip for the neighborhood near the school. Divide the class into pairs. Identify places to be walked to or near. Students should learn about the directions of these various places in the neighborhood from the school.

continued

Grid Pictures

Time Allotment: One or two class periods

Materials: Duplicated sheets, grid paper, crayons, markers

Grade Level: Elementary

Procedure: The use of grid pictures is an activity that will enable the students to use direction terms. Grid pictures require students to use grid lines to construct pictures.

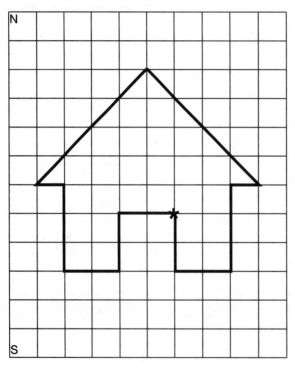

Directions:
Begin at "★" and go:
W-2; S-2; W-2;
N-3; W-1; NE-4;
SE-4; W-1; S-3;
W-2; N-2

You may now color your picture.

And the "Sun" Says

Time Allotment: Varied

Materials: Yard stick, marker to leave outdoors

Grade Level: Upper elementary and middle school

Procedure: Discuss the sun as an indicator of direction. Students are fascinated by this topic. The direction of shadows is an indicator that is easy for students to study, and

And the "Sun" Says **continued**

makes a logical starting place. The sun is always south of the United States so shadows are always pointed in a northerly direction. The sun always rises in the east and sets in the west, so morning shadows point in a northwesterly direction and afternoon ones in a north-easterly direction. Students can make these and other observations of the sun and its shadows as rough indicators of direction and can bring records of their observations to class for discussion.

Place the marker (i.e., any object large enough to cast a shadow) and record the direction and length of the shadow at various times during a given period of time. Variation: Divide the class into groups and have each group keep records on different markers around the school grounds.

Go "West"

Time Allotment: Varied

Materials: Direction signs

Grade Level: Elementary

Procedure: Most students are familiar with the game Simon Says. Label the class-room with cardinal directions (North, South, East, West), as well as intermediate directions (Northeast, Southeast, Southwest, Northwest). This will help students learn direction terms. The labels provide students with concrete reference points regarding directions. These can be reinforced through playing such games as Simon Says.

Paint the Playground

Time Allotment: Varied

Materials: Overhead projector, mural paper (or large butcher paper), paint (suitable for painting playground surface: white, red, yellow, blue, green), masking and clear adhesive tape, paint brushes

Grade Level: Middle school and elementary

Procedure: A huge map of the United States painted on your school's playground makes a great project. First divide the country into sections. Using a transparency and overhead projector, draw each section (divided into states) onto mural paper. A good size is about 20 feet by 30 feet (butcher paper may be taped together to use). Next have one crew of students take the map outside, a section at a time, and align and secure it with rocks or tape. Another group can paint around the entire outline of the map with white paint. When it is dry, assign each student one or more states to cut out of the original pattern and outline on the large painted map. States can then be painted red, green, yellow, and blue, and reoutlined in white with the names lettered on them. Students from elementary classes can also work on

Paint the Playground **continued**

states as teams and then fill in water and land boundaries. (Note: Check with local weather forecasts before starting this project. Parental volunteers may also be needed.)

Nobody Eats Shredded Wheat

Time Allotment: One class period

Materials: Transparency or chart, duplicated sheets, crayons, markers

Grade Level: Elementary

Procedure: Often it is difficult for students to remember the terms *North*, *East*, *South*, and *West* and how they usually are related to drawn maps. By using nmeonics, reinforce the terms by a simple phrase, "*Nobody Eats Shredded Wheat*," and an accompanying diagram, such as that shown in the example.

Nobody Eats Shredded Wheat **continued**

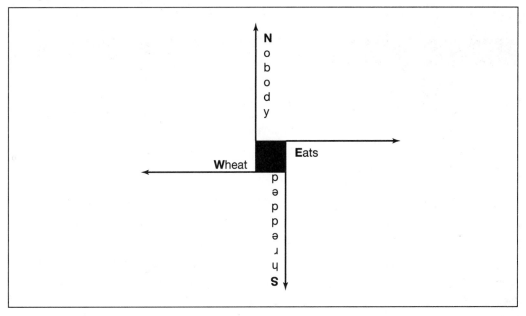

SYMBOLS

You are driving down the interstate. The green sign that gives the exit number and other information about the next exit is in full view. While you may be looking for the number, your youngster has already identified the "golden arches" and is begging to stop. Students deal with symbols on a daily basis, but they may not relate their experience to the term being used as a part of social studies instruction.

By definition, a symbol is a representation. Students in the lower elementary levels need experiences in comparing objects to their symbols. Three-dimensional classroom maps would certainly be helpful in providing appropriate learning experiences for students.

As students demonstrate an understanding of symbols, more abstract materials may be introduced, such as pictures or drawings. These are important in helping students understand that features may be represented by symbols. For example, pictures of lakes or rivers may be shown in certain ways on drawn maps, yet students understand that they look differently on actual photographs.

One major component of any map is the legend. On the legend, the representative symbols for cities, towns, rivers, mountains, or other information are presented. It is important that students be provided with experience in using the legend to find information on a map. It is equally important that students learn that one of the first steps to take in reading any map is familiarizing themselves with the legend.

ACTIVITIES

ACTIVITIES RELATED TO SYMBOL
And the "Sign" Says

Time Allotment: One or two class periods

Materials: Drawings or pictures of various signs, duplicated sheets of various signs, drawing paper, markers

Grade Level: Elementary

Procedure: Discuss the importance of signs (e.g., to tell us which direction to take, what may be ahead on the road or street, which door to go through). Show the students a

And the Sign Says

Directions: Identify each of the signs below. Then draw and describe two additional signs that were discussed in class.

Answer key: 1. stop, 2. telephone, 3. intersection, 4. school crossing, 5. railroad crossing, 6. bike route, 7. one way, 8. street sign, 9. yield.

And the "Sign" Says **continued**

number of familiar signs that are used generally on a national or international level. Following the discussion, students should identify the signs and markings on a duplicated sheet. In addition to those that you prepare, have a space for the students to add one or more that were mentioned in the discussion. Variation: Students may develop their own signs. They should also provide an explanation of why the sign is important and when or where it should be used.

Landscape Pictures

Time Allotment: One or two class periods

Materials: Paper, crayons, markers

Grade Level: Lower elementary and elementary

Procedure: Discuss symbols that could be used in landscape pictures: hills, mountains, roads, bridges, trees. Students decide what symbols should look like and draw them on a chart. Label symbols. Each student should draw a landscape picture using only symbols.

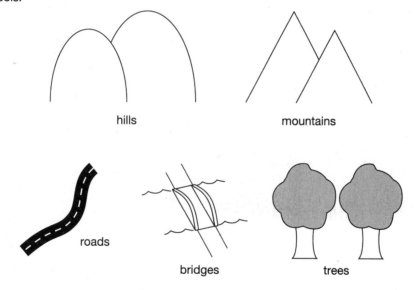

hills   mountains

roads

bridges   trees

Floor Plan

Time Allotment: Two or three class periods

Materials: Dollhouse furniture or small boxes to represent furniture, large drawing paper (or butcher paper), markers, pencils, pens

Grade Level: Elementary

Floor Plan **continued**

Procedure: Take a large piece of paper, place dollhouse furniture on it, and let the students examine it. Remove the objects and ask a student to replace them exactly as they were. This will probably prove to be very frustrating, if not impossible. Next, replace the articles and have students trace around them. Discuss use of symbols and how a floor plan is a simple map. Students should decide on symbols that are to be used to represent furniture. Finally, they should draw the floor plan using the symbols. Note: It is important that students understand that their floor plans may not be the same in any way except for the symbols used.

Picture vs. Symbol

Time Allotment: One or two class periods

Materials: Pictures (postcards are excellent), maps, magazines, scissors, glue

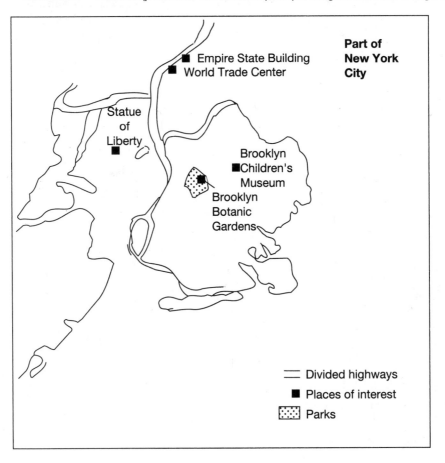

Picture vs. Symbol **continued**

Grade Level: Elementary

Procedure: Show the students a number of pictures. Then discuss how the picture may be represented by a certain symbol on a map. Have the students locate pictures of various places or things that are represented on maps. Then have students identify the various representations on the maps.

Draw A Shoe

Time Allotment: One class period

Materials: Drawing paper, pencils, markers, crayons

Grade Level: Elementary and middle school

Procedure: It is often difficult for students to understand the problems cartographers face in deciding which symbols should represent what objects on maps. It is also important that we keep in mind that cartographers have to draw maps of places as they look down from above. While this sounds easy, students will see the complexity involved when they attempt to be cartographers.

Students should attempt to draw their shoes by looking down. They will probably need to be reminded that they are only looking down, and should not draw the sides, etc.

(-----)ville, U.S.A.

Time Allotment: One or two class periods

Materials: Drawing paper, butcher paper, crayons, markers

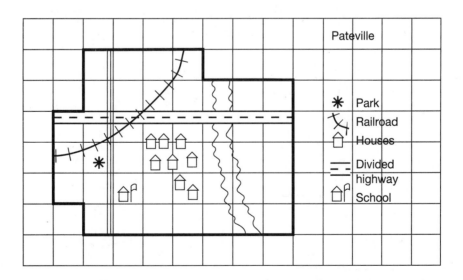

(-----)ville, U.S.A. **continued**

Grade Level: Elementary and middle school

Procedure: Students will enjoy demonstrating their understanding of symbols through developing their own maps. A pretend city or town may be developed by the students using information from their class and neighborhood. For example, the students might name certain locations after the local radio station or students in the class. Monuments, places, streets, etc. must be labeled with appropriate symbols. Students may develop individual maps and then combine them to make a large map of a new state. Note: The name of the city or town may be made up from the teacher's name or a student's name (e.g., Pateville, U.S.A.)

Contour Lines

Time Allotment: Two or three class periods

Materials: Cardboard, markers, different colors of modeling clay, reference materials

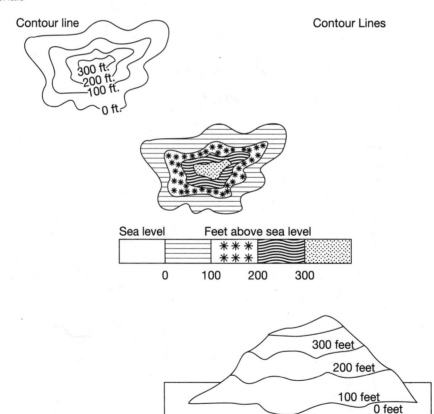

Contour Lines **continued**

> **Grade Level:**   Upper elementary and middle school
>
> **Procedure:**   When trying to show the height of the land, the method used is contour lines. These are lines that show the elevation of land from sea level.
>
> One way of helping students understand the concept of contour lines is to have them form land masses, using different colors of clay for each level. For example, using a map similar to the one in the example, students would develop a model of the mountain. Note: It is important that students have been introduced to the terms sea level and elevation prior to the hands-on experience.

LOCATION

The term location can probably best be defined with the answer to the question: Where is it? In map and globe skills, the term location deals with the ability of students to identify or locate certain places, areas, or routes of various kinds. Also, students should be able to use such terms as latitude and longitude in locating relative places.

In talking about location as a map and globe skill in social studies, it is important to provide students with experiences in using the information in meaningful ways. Relate the information to events seen or heard about on television or radio. Encourage a better understanding of where certain events are taking place by having students find or locate the area on a map.

One of the most memorable experiences of my life was the move from rural Pumpkin Center, Alabama, to Fairbanks, Alaska. It was made more enjoyable because my fourth grade teacher helped me learn to read maps well enough that I could understand the different locations we would be travelling through. While not all of our students have the opportunity for such a direct experience, through activities, films, and the use of pictures, we can provide vicarious experiences to encourage long-term learning.

ACTIVITIES

ACTIVITIES RELATED TO LOCATION
Locate the City

Time Allotment: One or two class periods

Locate the City **continued**

Materials: State maps (one for each student), social studies texts

Grade Level: Elementary

Procedure: The students should open their maps, on the desk or on the floor, so that they can see the whole map. Point out the letters and numbers (coordinates) along the sides of the map. Have students turn their maps over and look at the list of cities on the back with a letter and number after each name. The cities are listed in alphabetical order and the coordinates tell you where to find the city on the map. Note: Road maps may usually be obtained from the state highway director's office or department of tourism. Also, this activity may be modified to use with maps in social studies texts for more practice or if road maps are unavailable. Variation: After the students have gained some experience using coordinates, they may list cities on index cards and locate them on the map with a partner.

I-Spy

Time Allotment: One or two class periods

Materials: Two world wall maps, maps in social studies text

Grade Level: Elementary and middle school

Procedure: This activity is to reinforce or help students learn more about the location of countries. The teacher can either write the name of a country on the board or have the names of countries written on cards. The class may be divided into two teams or as a whole class one at a time identify or "spy" the location of the countries. The students should say "I spy _____" when they locate the country. Variation: This activity may be modified to focus on rivers, lakes, or major cities.

Treasure Map

Time Allotment: One or two class periods

Materials: Small objects to hide and find (e.g., treasures), drawing paper, pencils, crayons, markers

Grade Level: Upper elementary and middle school

Procedure: Treasure maps have a hidden or buried treasure and a set of directions designed to lead the hunter to the treasure. Students can be given maps of the classroom, school, or playground and directions leading them to a predetermined hiding place on the map. Variation: Students will also enjoy developing treasure maps they can share with classmates.

State Songs

Time Allotment: Varied

State Songs **continued**

Materials: Records or tapes, song books, musical instruments

Grade Level: Elementary

Procedure: Learning the names and locations of the 50 states can be a challenge for students. One fun way for them to learn the information, and have fun with songs at the same time, is through listening to or singing certain songs that mention particular states or parts of the country. Examples: "My Old Kentucky Home," "This Land Is Your Land," "Rocky Mountain High," "Deep in the Heart of Texas."

Where Is the News Taking Place?

Time Allotment: Varied

Materials: Various news periodicals (newspapers, magazines), scissors, wall-mounted world map, globe

Grade Level: Elementary and middle school

Procedure: Set aside one wall or bulletin board for current events in other countries around the world. Students should cut out, read, and write a short summary of news articles about events taking place. Each should be labeled and the location where they took place also labeled on the wall map or globe.

World Hunt

Time Allotment: One or two class periods

Materials: Newspaper and magazine clippings of names of countries and cities, reference books, maps, globe

Grade Level: Elementary and middle school

Procedure: Mount the newspaper names on the cards, then laminate or cover with clear contact paper. Have the students pretend they are going on a trip to the cities or countries named on their cards. Discuss with the students why it is necessary to find out about the places before they visit them—climate factors, customs, culture, and so on. Review latitude and longitude. Students should locate the necessary atlases, maps, or globes and begin their world hunt in search of the answers. Variation: This may be played as a game. If playing as a game, one point is given for each correct answer.

E.R.U. (Explorers-R-Us)

Time Allotment: One or two class periods

Materials: Writing paper, drawing paper, markers, crayons, pens, pencils

Grade Level: Middle school

E.R.U. (Explorers-R-Us) **continued**

> **Procedure:**   The students should be given the following directions.
>
> You are a world explorer for the famous company E.R.U. You have just discovered, after years of exploration, a section of the world that has never before been seen by human eyes. It is an awesome place, and you want to write a letter to E.R.U. telling them about it. (Remember that E.R.U. has paid your expenses for the past few years and they expect great things from you.) Your letter needs to be very accurate and include a lot of important information about your new discovery. Make sure you include the absolute location, relative location, hemisphere, and the landforms found there. This is your big break as an explorer so make the most of it! You will also want to include a sketch of your discovery.

SCALE

Recently the students from one of my classes were about to undertake field experiences at several different schools. As the placement coordinator was giving them their information packets, she told them that a map to each particular school would be in the packet. Quickly she added, "Leave early or make a trial run . . . our maps are not drawn to scale." After she left, there were a couple of students who asked what she meant. Obviously those students needed a review of basic skills they should have learned at the elementary, or at least at the middle school level.

In helping students develop a good understanding of the concept of scale, it is important to move from direct to more abstract experiences. First they need to develop an understanding of relative size. This may be accomplished by having students compare pictures or models with the large objects they represent, for example, a picture of a bus compared to the actual bus, a toy tree from a board game compared to a real tree outside the school.

As students develop an understanding of scale, they may begin to complete experiences with measuring by having one inch equal a yard and drawing a map of the classroom. Later, they may use a similar method by using math skills to determine how high a building is (e.g., 1 inch = 20 feet; the building model is 122 inches high).

Graphic or bar scales with segments numbered to show miles and a conversion of inches to miles can usually be found in social studies texts and accompanying material. The advantage of using these is that all students in a given group or class will have the same map and scale. This will enable the teacher to provide a great deal of whole or small group instruction and will provide the students with their individual maps.

Other materials are available from educational publishers that may be beneficial for helping students further their understanding of scale. It is also very appropriate for the teacher to design maps for the particular study he may be undertaking with a class.

FIGURE 3-1 Use the Scale

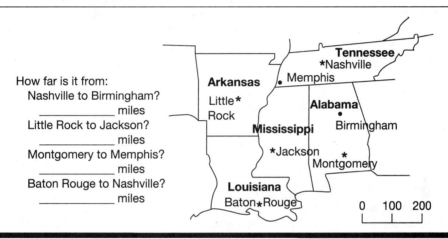

How far is it from:
Nashville to Birmingham?
_____ miles
Little Rock to Jackson?
_____ miles
Montgomery to Memphis?
_____ miles
Baton Rouge to Nashville?
_____ miles

ACTIVITIES

ACTIVITIES RELATED TO SCALE
Walk a Mile in My Shoes

Time Allotment: One or two class periods

Materials: Field trip permission, map of area of field trip, comfortable walking shoes

Grade Level: Elementary and middle school

Procedure: After introducing the concept of distance and mile as a measurement, have the students go on a field trip. As a part of the field trip, they should walk a square mile. After walking the mile, they should look at the map and notice, specifically, the scale of one mile. This will surely help develop an understanding of the concept of scale.

Alaska or Texas: Which is Really the Largest?

Time Allotment: One or two class periods

Alaska or Texas: Which is Really the Largest? **continued**

Materials: Various maps of the United States, measuring strips or rulers

Grade Level: Elementary

Procedure: Sometimes cartographers combine more than one scale on a map. Often a smaller scale is used for Alaska and a larger scale for the other 48 states. This confuses students when they are told that Alaska is larger than Texas even though it appears smaller on the map. Using the scale on a number of maps, students should compare the sizes of the two states. Variation: Students may measure the states by using only one scale and then explain why this would be a problem for anyone who didn't understand why two scales are necessary.

More Scale: More Detail

Time Allotment: One or two class periods

Materials: Various maps, social studies texts, resource materials, reference materials

Grade Level: Elementary and middle school

Procedure: Explain to students that small scale maps are used to show large areas and large scale maps are used to show small areas in textbooks, atlases, and other sources. Have the students describe the features and greater details shown on large scale maps that cannot be shown on small scale maps. Variation: Students may draw their own maps of areas by different scales and compare.

Comparison of Our State With Others

Time Allotment: One or two class periods

Materials: Transparencies of states to be studied, duplicated sheets for students (or inexpensive overlays), pens for writing on transparencies or markers for sheets, reference materials (e.g., atlases, road maps)

Grade Level: Elementary and middle school

Procedure: Make a base transparency from an outline map of the United States or a section of the United States. Highlight your state. Then prepare overlays showing the surrounding states. By introducing the states one at a time, the size of the states may be compared. If you make separate overlays, be sure each map has the same scale.

As you make the comparison using the overhead projector, students may make various maps on duplicated sheets or drawing paper, or you may use inexpensive sheet protectors so that they may make their own overlays for their base map. Variation: This activity can also be modified to be used with a study of countries.

continued

How Big Is Our Classroom

Time Allotment: One or two class periods

Materials: Drawing paper, markers, rulers, various materials to use as measuring tools

Grade Level: Elementary

Procedure: In order to help students develop a better understanding of scale, have the class divide into groups. Next, they should identify the measuring tool they will use as their scale base. For example, a ruler, a given textbook, a gem clip, the chalkboard eraser. Next the students should develop and draw their map of the classroom. Finally, the students should exchange drawings of the classroom and try to figure out the size of the room.

Finding the Distance on A Map

Time Allotment: One or two class periods

Materials: Duplicated sheets, various maps, pencils

Finding Distance on a Map

Directions: Finding a distance on a map is very easy as long as you have what is called a distance scale on the map. Look at the small map of lower California below. How far is it from Los Angeles to San Diego?

Without a map scale you have no way of knowing this without actually going to California to measure it or looking up the information in a book.

If this illustration was added to the map you could then measure the distance on the map and get a rough estimate of the distance between the two cities.

60 miles

Using the same map, find the list of pairs of cities. See how closely you can estimate the distance between those cities using the scale on the map. Use another small piece of paper if you need to retrace the scale so you can move it about.

Finding the Distance on a Map **continued**

Grade Level: Elementary

Procedure: In explaining to students the usefulness of a scale, practice is needed with various types of maps. It is also important that students understand that a rough estimate of the number of miles between two places may be obtained by using the scale. Lessons such as the example may be used.

Drawing a Map to Scale

Time Allotment: One or class period

Materials: Grid paper, pencils, reference materials showing maps

Grade Level: Elementary and middle school

Procedure: Have students draw a map onto a piece of grid paper. Then using a piece of grid paper with larger squares, they should draw the same map again. This will reinforce the idea of the difference between maps and scale on maps.

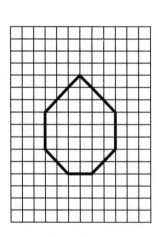 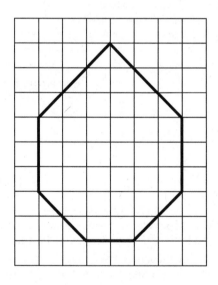

HELPFUL HINTS FOR UNIT 3:

1. Select three of the activities from this unit. How would you modify these to be more appropriate for students you may be working with?
2. In looking back at your school experiences, what do you remember about map and globe skills?
3. Working with senior citizens as a part of learning about a community is suggested as an activity. Design and conduct your own Senior Citizen Interview. Share your findings with those of the class. (Note: You may want to ask questions about their school experiences related to social studies!)
4. Make a collection of various maps that you may need in helping students learn certain skills. Share your collection with your peers.
5. Review the map and globe skills mentioned in Unit Three. Are there any that you feel you need to improve on? If so, work through the activities related to that area, and find three other activities to help you improve your background of knowledge and experience.

REFERENCES

Barr, R., Barth, J., & Shermis, S. (1977). *Defining the social studies*, Bulletin 51. Arlington, VA: National Council for the Social Studies.

Committee on Geographic Education, National Council for Geographic Education, and Association of American Geographers. (1984). *Guidelines for geographic education: Elementary and secondary schools.* Washington, DC, and Macombe, IL: National Council for Geographic Education and Association of American Geographers.

STUDY QUESTIONS FOR UNIT 4:   1. What areas are traditionally included in the language arts curriculum? **2.** How important are trade books as a part of social studies instruction?   **3.** How can we encourage students not to read their oral reports?   **4.** Why are simulations valuable learning experiences for students? **5.** How much time do we really spend helping our students learn how to listen?   **6.** Should writing be important in social studies class, or should we teach those skills only during language arts?

INTRODUCTION One area of the traditional elementary or middle school curriculum that we often ask

Language Arts and Social Studies

education students to note as they visit or complete practicums in real classrooms is the area of language arts. We ask them to look for various types of learner activities and to look for the types of materials available for learner and instructor use. At times, we may ask education students to identify instructional strategies that may be employed by educators during language arts instruction. Finally, we provide a definition of language arts for our students.

The language arts curriculum may be traditionally defined as the study of the areas of reading, speaking, writing, and listening. A block of the school day may be focused on instruction in these areas, specifically dealing with the skills needed by students for positive growth in literacy. While the need for skills instruction may be a point of contention between various educators, the fact that each of the areas of language is an integral part of the total curriculum—and school experience—is commonly accepted.

In considering the various discipline areas in the total curriculum, one area in which language arts could (or possibly should) play a major role is the area of social studies. Embellishment of information that is often included as a part of social studies instruction may be accomplished more successfully through the integration of the components of language arts in meaningful activities that are based on learner involvement.

This unit will provide a discussion of strategies that may be implemented to integrate various components of language arts into social studies in meaningful and useful ways.

LITERATURE AND TRADE BOOKS

One of the stories I remember my dad halfway telling and halfway reading was a story about Davey Crockett. Another intriguing story was about the tragedy of the Titanic. Later, I remember my older sister having to write a book report on *Anne Frank: The Diary of a Young Girl* and I enjoyed reading bits and pieces of the book, which was, of course, not on our class reading list.

Although not related directly to social studies class, the memories of dealing with various forms of printed materials can help establish a basis for the use of literature as a part of social studies instruction. Student memories should be inventoried for past experiences with any form of print. A print-rich environment should not be limited to lower elementary or primary grade levels but should extend throughout the school experience, especially in the upper elementary and middle school levels.

Students beginning at grade levels where social studies content texts are widely used may begin to demonstrate some level of difficulty with reading. Although there may be a number of reasons for the problem, one that must be considered by the teacher is the vocabulary often found in text materials. For example, upon hearing or reading the phrase "race for office" students may conjure up visions of an auto race or track tournament. The vocabulary found in content area texts sometimes is not the same as in everyday conversation.

Some students find information in textbooks to be dull or dry because of the types of information discussed or because of the style of presentation. Materials used in social studies are generally written in expository style, which can be so succinct that students do not grasp the relationships between the material and their lives or the importance of learning the information (Burns, Roe, & Ross, 1992).

There has been much improvement, with textbooks becoming more student-oriented, but it is still important that teachers be aware of the possibility of difficulty, and aware of methods of providing for the learning needs of students. One source of materials for teachers is literature, or more specifically, trade books. The use of high interest trade books along with the texts will help students make the transition into the more difficult expository textbooks and help make the information more meaningful.

Trade books are fiction or nonfiction books that are available to the general public (e.g., library books). Although students may read trade books for pleasure, the books may also be read to gain information on specific topics. In addition, trade books may be used by students when the adopted or available textbooks are not sufficient, as when the student does not read on the prescribed level or reads above the level. When considering the various types of trade books, it is important that we as educators develop a working knowledge of the materials appropriate for use by those students with whom we come in contact every day.

In order to decide on appropriate children's literature or trade books for use in the social studies classroom, the teacher should become familiar with those suggested by the Joint Committee of the National Council for the Social Studies (NCSS) and the Children's Book Council. An annotated list of their suggestions is found in each spring issue of *Social Education*. The list contains books that "(1) are written for children K-8; (2) emphasize human relations; (3) present an original or fresh theme or a fresh slant on a traditional topic; (4) are highly readable; and, when appropriate, (5) include maps and illustrations" ("Notable 1990 Children's Tradebooks," 1991). This list, along with others provided by professional organizations, may provide suggestions, but it is up to the classroom teacher and school media specialist to decide when use of the materials would be appropriate.

In order for the classroom teacher to decide what is most appropriate, the following suggestions may be implemented: (1) identify the concepts for further development; (2) locate the appropriate trade books that will teach these concepts; (3) present the books to the students through read-aloud sessions, tapes, or copies for independent reading; (4) use trade books to accompany the text reading (i.e., help students develop an understanding of *why* the information is related to the text and vice versa); and (5) provide extension or ongoing activities to reinforce the information (Brozo & Tomlinson, 1986).

In deciding on the activities to use in conjunction with trade books, it is again the responsibility of the classroom teacher to relate the activities to social studies information. For example, students need to understand that although stories and dramatic activities add life to facts, they may not be completely true. Accuracy of dates, places, and key names must be emphasized. In deciding on materials to use as sources during activities, teachers need to help students learn to check reference books, as well as the bibliography of trade books, if provided (Storey, 1982; Zarnowski, 1988).

Finally, in social studies as with other areas of the curriculum, prior to implementation of activities, discussion should take place that will help students see the connection between what they are studying in the text-book and what they are doing in the activity. Activities should not be undertaken just to take up time but should have a purpose—a meaning-ful goal that should help students develop a greater understanding.

ACTIVITIES

ACTIVITIES RELATED TO LITERATURE AND TRADE BOOKS
Unnamed Biographies

Time Allotment: One or two class periods

Materials: Short biographies

Grade Level: Elementary

Procedure: Read short biographies of well-known people related to information the class is studying. Do not mention any names. Have the students guess the identity of each person described in the biographies.

continued

Important Character

Time Allotment: Varied

Materials: Story

Grade Level: Elementary and middle school

Procedure: Have the students listen to a story to determine which character is most important to the story. Ask each student to write her choice on a slip of paper. Place all the slips in a bowl. Draw from the bowl and ask students to explain their choices. Variation: Chart the responses. Compare the number of students who felt certain characters were most important.

Poetry Readings

Time Allotment: One or two class periods

Materials: Collection of appropriate poems

Grade Level: Upper elementary and middle school

Procedure: Have students read or read to them poems that are likely to evoke feelings, moods, and emotions. Encourage the students to discuss how a poem makes them feel and have them try to identify why the poem affects them that way.

Time Line

Time Allotment: Two or three class periods

Materials: Butcher paper, markers, crayons, book

Grade Level: Upper elementary and middle school

Procedure: After the class has either read a book or had a book read to them, divide them into small groups. Ask the students to draw a line across a piece of paper to represent the span of time covered in their group's chapter or section of the book. Then they should divide the line into segments of time, with the dates written below the line and an illustration of what happened on that date above the line.

This Is My Story

Time Allotment: Two or three class periods

Materials: Stories, paper, pencils

Grade Level: Upper elementary and middle school

This is My Story **continued**

> **Procedure:**   After students have read a particular story, ask them to pretend they are a character in the story. They should write a log or diary describing the events in the story from the selected character's point of view.

Dramatic Book Report

Time Allotment: Two or three class periods

Materials: Stories, pencils, paper, props (according to need)

Grade Level: Elementary and middle school

Procedure: Divide the class into groups. Each group should develop a dramatization of a part of the book or story they have read. Students should be encouraged to be creative in their presentation.

Part II

Time Allotment: Varied

Materials: Books, pens, pencils, paper, dictionaries, thesauruses, markers, crayons

Grade Level: Middle school

Procedure: After students have read books, they should then write a sequel or another adventure for the main character. Students should include appropriate illustrations. These may be placed in the class library for sharing or shared through presentations.

Book Jackets

Time Allotment: One or two class periods

Materials: Books, paper, markers, crayons, pens, pencils, reference materials

Grade Level: Elementary

Procedure: Students may design book jackets for their favorite books. A brief summary of the story is written on the front inside flap and a short sketch of the author on the back inside flap. The student-made book jackets may be displayed as part of a bulletin board to encourage others to read the books.

Book Report Collage

Time Allotment: Two or three class periods

Materials: Magazines, scissors, glue, markers, pens, pencils, butcher or manila drawing paper

Book Report Collage **continued**

Grade Level: Elementary

Procedure: Students should cut pictures from magazines to illustrate the information in the book they have read. They should glue the pictures on a large piece of paper to form a collage. Finally, they should cut out letters to make the title of the book and paste it boldly across the collage. Variation: Students may write captions for each picture.

Book Boxes

Time Allotment: Varied

Materials: Boxes of various sizes, contact paper, magazines, varied books, pens, paper, pencils, markers, construction paper

Grade Level: Upper elementary and middle school

Procedure: Focusing on a particular unit or theme of study, have the students develop book boxes that may be shared with classmates. To make a book box, select the topic and have students locate several books related to the topic. They should also plan activities appropriate for the books and put those in the box. Other items that might be included are bookmarks, games, or puzzles that go along with the topic. Variation: Older students may work in pairs to develop book boxes for younger students.

ORAL REPORTS

Once I taught at a school where oral reports were an expectation. Trying to accommodate those expectations, I dutifully assigned topics to students. The first set of reports went off with moderate success. On day two of the reports, the first young man stammered and gasped and clung to the corner of my desk until his knuckles were turning a lighter shade of pale. Fearing he would collapse at any second, I thanked him for his wonderful report before he was finished with the first few paragraphs and asked him to return to his chair.

It is quite possible that many of us can identify with this student either through personal experience or by memories of peers or former students with whom we have silently suffered as they gave a report. In many classrooms, students are still expected to give reports. The goal of reports is to provide individuals or small groups with a means for sharing information gathered on a particular topic. Unfortunately, the downfall of many oral reports is that students more or less copy their report from a reference book (e.g., an encyclopedia), which leads to mispronunciation of words and a general loss of meaning for the presenter and total boredom for the audience.

It is important for students to recognize that what they have to say is important. Students need to receive guidance and support in every step of development of skills that will enable them to give an effective presentation. Students in today's elementary and middle school social studies classes arrive with greater skills in oral reporting than those students in the last decade or two. These skills come into focus because they are ever-growing survival skills for our students. According to McClure (1989) and Collins (1992), the students of today know how to effectively persuade, inform, and entertain.

Students need to learn how to use these strategies effectively, not only in their everyday conversations but also in presentations. According to Block (1993), students need to be able to learn how to speak effectively, as this will become (if it is not already) the main method for communication for them personally and professionally. Research has shown that students who are not provided with opportunities and successes in the development of oral abilities will have less development in other areas, such as reading and writing (Loban, 1976; Sampson, 1986).

Although the composition is a major aspect of the report, the delivery or presentation is equally important. It is important that the teacher establish the guidelines for the presentation and let students know what is expected. In addition, student involvement in decision making about the reports can be beneficial. For example, elementary and middle school students who have had a number of experiences with reports may be able to offer suggestions concerning the strategies that have worked for them.

General guidelines for students presenting individual reports could include:

1. Know your topic.
2. Begin your report with an attention grabber.
3. Use vocabulary that *you* understand.
4. Speak clearly and loudly.
5. Use graphic aids if appropriate.
6. Look at your audience.
7. Practice before giving your report.
8. Be prepared to answer questions about your report.

At times a report prepared and presented by a small group of students may be more appropriate, so guidelines for group formation, participation, and presentation may also need to be developed.

Group formation:

1. Identify the purpose of the report.
2. Determine group size 3–6 members.
3. Establish the group members' roles.
4. Establish conflict resolution strategies.
5. Determine time allotment.

Group participation:

1. Group member roles (e.g., leader, recorder, reporter)
2. Aim of report
3. Materials needed (e.g., reference materials, graphic aids)
4. Method of presentation

Group presentation:

1. Who will present? (one person, take turns)
2. How will presentation be made? (standing, table, skit) A small group plan might be graphically represented such as shown in Figure 4-1.

FIGURE 4-1 Graphic Plan for Small Group Work

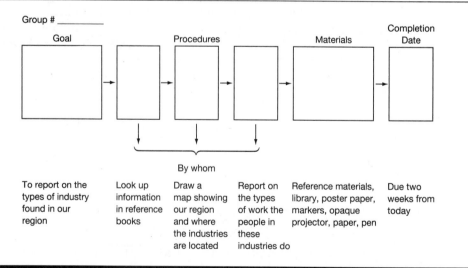

ACTIVITIES

ACTIVITIES RELATED TO ORAL REPORTS
Listen to the Radio

Time Allotment: One or two class periods

Materials: Cassette tapes of appropriate radio shows, checklist, cassette player, pen, pencil

Grade Level: Upper elementary and middle school

Procedure: Speaking and listening share a number of characteristics. When listening, one is not simply hearing uttered sounds but using voice quality, inflection, and expression in order to interpret the intended message.

Students should listen to two radio shows carefully, then make a comparison of the speakers' presentation styles. This may be accomplished by using a checklist such as the one shown.

Presentation Checklist

Rating scale: 1 = below average   2 = average   3 = above average
                4 = outstanding   5 = not observed

Speaker One		Speaker Two	
1. Voice		1. Voice	
2. Speech		2. Speech	
3. Energy		3. Energy	
4. Ability to hold interest		4. Ability to hold interest	
5. Purpose of speech clear		5. Purpose of speech clear	
6. Expression		6. Expression	
7. Voice level		7. Voice level	
8. Grammar		8. Grammar	

continued

For Presentation

Time Allotment:　Varied

Materials:　Written report on given topic, transparency, pen, overhead projector, screen

Grade Level:　Upper elementary and middle school

Procedure:　After writing a report, students may be asked to share with a group or whole class in a traditional manner. In order to help keep the class focused, the presenter may develop a sequential outline and refer to the outline (on a transparency and for use with the overhead projector). Variation: If more feasible, copies of the outline might be made so that each student will have a copy. Also, transparencies of characters or other information from the report may be put into chart form and used to enhance class participation and understanding during the presentation.

The Expert Says

Time Allotment:　Three or four class periods

Materials:　Interview form, possibly cassette recorder and tape, or video recorder and tape, pen, pencils

Grade Level:　Upper elementary and middle school

Procedure:　After students have given oral reports, or prepared written reports, partners may be chosen. The interviewer will ask the "expert" questions about the selected topic. After this session is completed the tape may be observed or listened to for reflection.

The Real Thing

Time Allotment:　Varied

Materials:　Artifacts, relics, table

Grade Level:　Elementary and middle school

Procedure:　The student should bring to class artifacts or relics to serve as the basis of the report being given. (NOTE: Parental permission or notification is recommended!)

The presenter should use the materials as a part of the actual presentation, and some of them may be passed around for closer observation following the report.

Today I Am . . .

Time Allotment:　One or two class periods

Materials:　Student-made costumes

Today I Am . . . **continued**

Grade Level: Elementary

Procedure: In giving an oral report about a famous person, students may be encouraged to dress the part of the person on whom they are reporting. This will provide a means for focusing attention of the rest of the class. A variation would be for students to give the report, in full costume, without identifying who it is about and have classmates guess after the report is completed.

"Silent" Movies

Time Allotment: Varied

Materials: Videos of appropriate movies, video player

Grade Level: Upper elementary and middle school

Procedure: Students will learn the relationship between factual presentation and fiction by developing and completing a narration for a video with the sound turned off. Students may later compare their narration with the dialogue of the actual video.

NOTE: Some movies, although historically factual or interesting, may not be suitable for classroom use. Preview carefully.

Today We Will Be Touring . . .

Time Allotment: Two or three class periods

Materials: Magazines, travel brochures, scissors, glue, paper for mounting (butcher or manila drawing), maps

Grade Level: Elementary and middle school

Procedure: Students should prepare a poster or collage of a specific area to be discussed. Then they may pretend to be tour guides and lead the class on a visit through the area (e.g., geographic location, historical landmark, city, town).

Today's News

Time Allotment: Varied

Materials: Reference materials, video camera, tape

Grade Level: Elementary and middle school

Procedure: Students may role-play the part of a newscaster making an on-the-spot report. The news may be a topic of current interest or the report may be related to an event from history. By videotaping, the class may enjoy the various on-the-spot reports at a later time or during a newscast.

Social Studies: Applications for a New Century

continued

Creative Drama

Time Allotment: Varied

Materials: Reference materials, paper, pens, pencils, props

Grade Level: Elementary and middle school

Procedure: Students may use dramatization to act out a particular event or sequence of events relating to the topic of study. Important facts should be included in the dramatization.

Puppets as Props or Characters

Time Allotment: Varied

Materials: Prepared skit or report, puppets, puppet stage

Grade Level: Lower and upper elementary

Procedure: One or more students may present information using puppets. The puppets used should represent figures or characters important to the topic.

SIMULATIONS

Simulations are activities that provide students with opportunities to explore real life situations. In simulations, at the elementary and middle school levels, students may explore issues and information, some of which are unsafe or less than feasible in real life.

Most students enjoy simulations and are highly motivated to be active participants. Although there is some discussion about the reasons for the high levels of motivation (Jarolimek, 1993; Michaelis, 1992), the results of simulations seem to be more advantageous than not. (See Table 4-1.)

High levels of motivation by students in simulations tend to be related to the natural curiosity of students. They tend to want to know *why* something is the way it is. For example, why we have empty apartment buildings in most cities, yet people are living in their cars or on the street. Because simulations deal with realistic situations and are not traditionally text-based, the level of learner involvement is high. As most teachers will probably agree, the more involved the learner, the more true learning will take place.

TABLE 4-1 Simulations: Advantages and Disadvantages

Advantages	Disadvantages
Positive attitude	Preparation required
Improve motivation	Time factor (in class)
Curiosity	Not parallel with teaching style
Creativity	Competition
Challenges	May be too simplistic or too complex
Problem solving and decision making	
Based on reality	

Teachers often find that the positive aspects of using simulations in the classroom far outweigh the negative. However, there are disadvantages that need to be addressed prior to undertaking the implementation of simulations as a teaching strategy. A major area for investigation involves the parallel of the teaching style normally used and that needed in order to implement simulations successfully. In simulations, the learner is at the center of the lesson rather than the teacher, as in many traditional teaching strategies. The amount of movement, student interaction, noise level, and general ambiguity with which the teacher is comfortable comes into play with the effectiveness of simulations in the classroom.

Teachers also need to consider the preparation required for simulations. Traditional teacher-directed lessons usually require less preparation than learner involvement lessons. It is important to note, however, that although simulations are probably very advantageous for learners, in order to meet the learning needs of all students, teachers would want to vary teaching strategies so that simulations would not be used every day. Information that might best be taught through the use of simulations would vary from class to class, with use being determined by the teacher.

In addition to the preparation, there is an extra amount of time needed in the class setting for implementation of simulations. Again, the goals that are being targeted for the class need to be evaluated in terms of the strategies that are implemented. For example, if covering the content is the goal, the use of simulations may not be as appropriate as other teaching strategies. On the other hand, if decision making and the development of problem solving skills are sought through instruction, then the teacher may want to consider the use of simulations.

One reason some teachers avoid using simulations is because of the competition that students may take very seriously. The desire to win can become such a focus that it leaves students feeling discouraged if they do not do well. This is of extreme importance for teachers working with preadolescents in upper elementary or middle school levels, as their self-concept is closely related to peer pressure. Students may need to be reminded that the emphasis of a simulation is learning.

The simulation basically is to help students become actively involved in learning about a real life experience or situation. Because of the complexity of real life, it is important that the teacher be aware of the possible complexity of simulations. A simulation should be realistic and simple enough to complete without losing its value as a valid learning experience. The final decision for implementation of simulations, as with any teaching strategy, must be made by the classroom teacher based on his knowledge about the needs and abilities of the class.

There are many commercial simulations available (see Table 4-2), but those that are designed for a particular class based on interests, needs, and abilities of the students will probably be most useful. Planning a simulation may be challenging or even overwhelming because of the complexity. Guidelines that might be suggested for planning include:

TABLE 4-2 Simulations Available Commercially

Title	Publisher
Access	Simile II
Amigos	Interact
Auction to Apathy	*Teacher* (Sept., 1972)
Boxcars	Interact
Chow	Interact
Code	Interact
Culture Contact	EMI
Dinosaur	Interact
Down with the King	Seabury
Empathy	Interact
Equality	Interact
Fire	Interact
Gingerbread Men	SS Strategies
Gold Rush Days	Edu-Game
How a Bill Becomes A Law	Muir
Beginning of Trade	SS Strategies
New City Telephone Company	Simile II

SOURCES
Interact, P.O. Box 262, Lakeside, CA 92040
EMI, P.O. Box 4272, Madison, WI 53711
Edu-Game, P.O. Box 1144, Sun Valley, CA 91352
Simile II, P.O. Box 910, Del Mar, CA 92014
Seabury Service Center, Somers, CT 06071
SS Strategies, Educational Insights, 150 W. Carob St., Compton, CA 90220

1. Purpose—What is going to be taught through implementation?
2. Scope—What is the issue? location? date (i.e., past, present, future)?
3. Roles—What function will each student have?
4. Resources—What resources will be dealt with? Will students deal with resources on an individual or group basis?
5. Sequence—Will the experience be one continuous action, or will the experience be divided into sections with evaluation taking place at the end of each division?
6. Rules for participants—Will there be identified leaders? How much movement will be necessary? Will there be rules for interaction during the simulation?
7. Overall evaluation—What will be the basis for success in relationship to the experience?

At the upper elementary and middle school levels, active learner involvement in testing or evaluating the overall premise of a simulation is encouraged. This will help the teacher and class decide on revisions needed in order to make a simulation more useful for a specific group of learners.

ACTIVITIES

ACTIVITIES RELATED TO SIMULATIONS
In the News

Time Allotment: Varied

Materials: News reports, taped news programs, video recorder, video player, paper, pencils, pens

Grade Level: Elementary and middle school

Procedure: The issue to be covered should be decided on based on the issues of current focus at the local or national levels. The number of students to be actively involved will vary; however, some of the roles to be considered include:

1. Anchorperson
2. In-the-field reporters
3. Camera persons
4. Research assistants

Each student or small group of students will be responsible for developing each report. The broadcast should be rehearsed. Finally, if possible, the group should deliver their presentation and, if possible, videotape and review.

continued

A New Island

Time Allotment: Varied

Materials: Chart paper, reference materials, paper, pens, markers

Grade Level: Elementary and middle school

Procedure: Students should focus their attention on how best to develop a new island that has been discovered in the _____ Ocean. It is a tropical paradise island with rocky beaches on one side and sandy beaches on the other; there are no native inhabitants.

The roles of the group members could include:

Governor or leader
City and community planners
Agricultural and forestry consultants
Industry representatives

Park Possible

Time Allotment: Varied

Materials: Chart paper, markers, pens, pencils, writing paper

Grade Level: Elementary

Procedure: The students at _____ Elementary School have played on an empty field as long as any of the students can remember. Although equipment has been installed in a number of parks developed around the city, the field has remained a place where high grass is cut once a year and trash is occasionally picked up by the city. In the last few years, more and more homeless people have set up tents and boxes in the field.

The students want to accommodate the needs of the homeless, but at the same time they want equipment installed and the grass cut so that they will have a real park in which to play.

Roles of group members might include:

Letter writing committee
Neighborhood survey takers
Cartographers (to develop maps of what the lot looks like today and what the lot could look like as a park and place for the homeless)

WRITTEN REPORTS

In a number of primary level classrooms, one of the opening activities of the day is often the development of a language experience story or report about current affairs in the community or happenings in the lives of students. Seemingly all of the students are anxious to see "their" information in writing. On the other hand, students in the upper elementary and middle school levels cringe and procrastinate upon being asked to prepare a written report. The reasons that students become less than positive about report writing are varied, but one suggestion is that they are not provided with ample instruction on the preparation of a written report.

One of the problems encountered is that students do not relate the writing process learned in language arts period with writing in other areas. There are many ways of describing the aspects of the writing process (Atwell, 1990; Calkins, 1986), but in general there are five stages that written reports should go through as the final product is developed. These are prewriting, drafting, revising, editing, and sharing.

In prewriting, students brainstorm, develop lists, gather information and read about the topic, make an outline, and think about the audience for whom they are writing. After initially planning the report, the students move to the second stage, drafting.

During the drafting stage, students should write as much as they can without being concerned about spelling or the mechanics of writing. Students should write what they think or what they have learned.

Some students will be ready to keep writing, and others may prefer to set aside their work for a period of time (e.g., a day or two) and then work on the third stage, revision. In this stage students may ask friends to read their reports. An area they may want to review includes the organization of information. They may also want to review the material to see if they need to add or delete material in order to make their reports more meaningful.

When the students have revised to the point that they feel their reports are meaningful, then they are ready to move to the editing stage. This is important because it includes checking spelling, punctuation, and grammar.

Finally, the report should be prepared for the last stage, sharing. Students should make a final copy. The final copy should be reviewed by the students so that all corrections or changes made during editing have been included. The final copy is then shared with peers, the teacher, or whomever was identified as the audience during the prewriting stage.

Although the stages for developing a written report seem simple, it is important that educators provide explanations and experiences for students. It is important for students to understand that the five stages are interrelated; that is, one does not always move stepwise from one stage to the next. Even during the editing stage writers sometimes discover areas where revision or additional information is needed. Because of this, whole-group experiences may be provided to explain or model the stages for development of a written report. Later the students may use these experiences while writing the reports independently.

One of the most difficult tasks for students in undertaking a project, especially a written report, is getting started. As a part of prewriting, brainstorming is important. A number of strategies are available, but two that especially encourage and motivate because students are so actively involved are *semantic mapping* and *KWL* (what we *k*now, what we *w*ant to learn, and what we have *l*earned) (Ogle, 1986). Both of these strategies focus on the use of prior knowledge as a starting point for locating and gathering information.

Semantic mapping (also sometimes referred to as semantic webbing) is an informal technique for helping students brainstorm about a topic. As described in Unit One (see Figure 1-6), even younger students can learn to organize their thoughts or information by using semantic mapping.

There are many types of maps that may be used. Three basic formats are the basic semantic map, the descriptive map, and the sequential map.

FIGURE 4-2 Basic Semantic Map

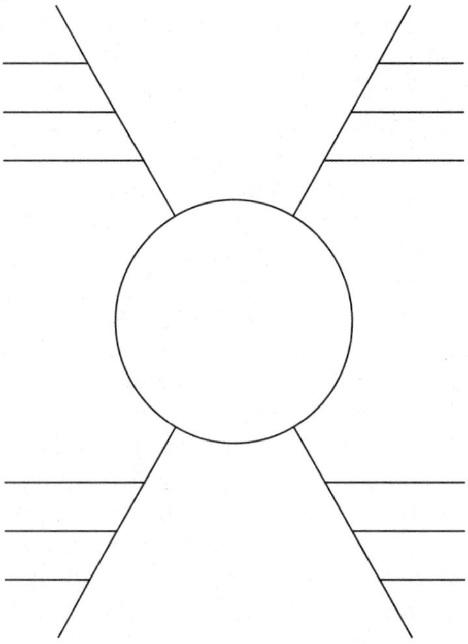

FIGURE 4-3 Descriptive Map

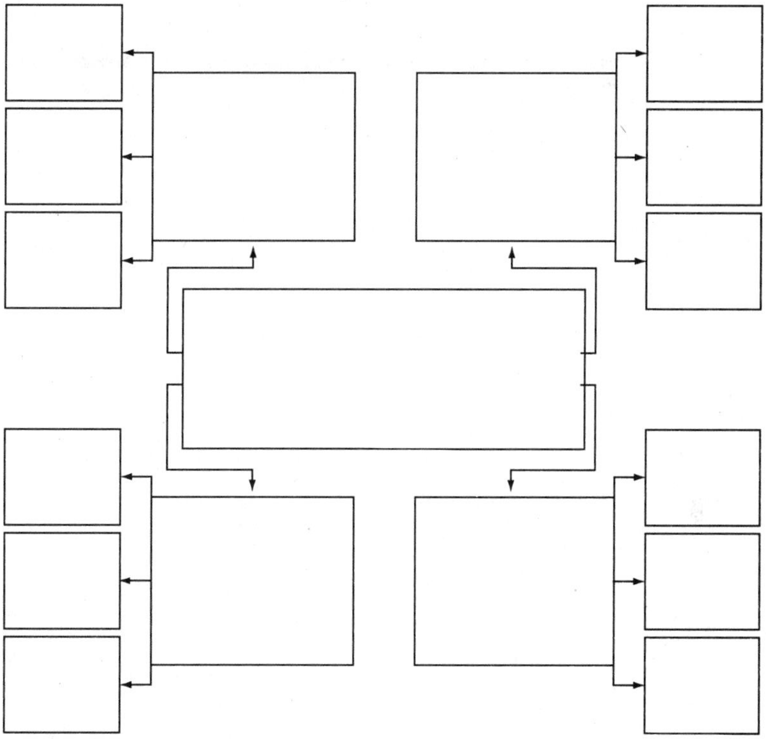

All share common characteristics but differ in format and organization of ideas.

The basic semantic map provides students with a very skeletal outline of a topic. (See Figure 4-2.) The topic or concept is placed in the center circle. On each of the arms a main idea or subconcept is written. Each main idea will have a number of supporting facts that are placed appropriately.

The descriptive map is especially useful in the area of social studies when two or more characteristics or main ideas of a topic are being described or compared. (See Figure 4-3.) As shown in the example, this helps students to develop questions they may want to investigate in their written reports. It also helps them to organize information for easier writing.

A third mapping technique that may be used as students prepare a written report in social studies is the sequential map. (See Figure 4-4.) Because the area of social studies, especially the historical area, deals with

FIGURE 4-4 Sequential Map

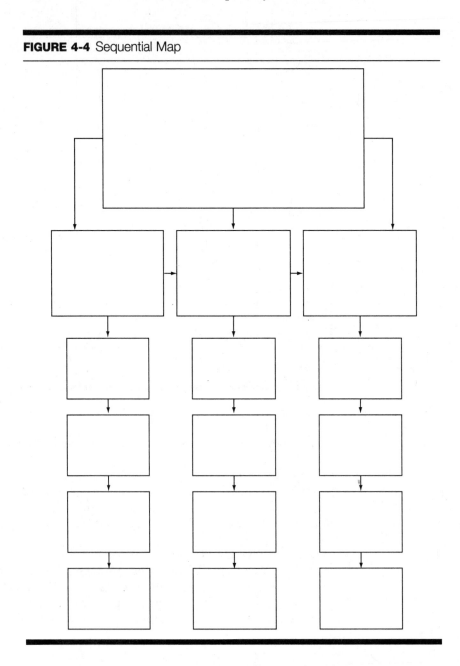

FIGURE 4-5 K-W-L Basic Format

K (Know)	W (Want to know)	L (Learned)

the complex concept of time, students often need a way to help them organize information in sequential order. By using a sequential map, students may organize any number of areas or sub-concepts under a general topic, and also may see how they relate to one another if the topic requires such a comparison.

There are many types of mapping activities that may be used, but it is important that we encourage modification to meet the individual needs of students. The maps may be made larger so that more information may be included, or kept very simple for more general types of reports. In any situation, the beginning purpose of using mapping is to help students use their prior knowledge as well as focus on a topic.

Another strategy for helping students think or brainstorm about a topic is the KWL (know, want to learn, learned). This strategy was developed by Ogle (1986) as a means of helping students with organization of thoughts, individually or as a group. In this strategy, students first brainstorm and list everything they know about a particular topic. In the second step, students develop questions on the topic about which they

FIGURE 4-6 What the Students Know about a Topic

K (Know)	W (Want to know)	L (Learned)
had ceremonies ate berries lived in America		

would like to learn more. The third stage of the strategy is for students to list what they have learned about a topic after they have completed their research. This strategy is especially useful because it encourages organization of thoughts. Again, as with mapping, the KWL strategy may be modified based on the students' needs as well as the topic for more or less detail.

After the initial stage of brainstorming is completed, some type of information-gathering technique must be implemented. For a large number of us, during out elementary and middle school years (and unfortunately up through the college years for some people) this meant going to the encyclopedia and copying our report. Of course we did this (and many of our students still do this) because (1) we waited until the last minute and (2) we had no earthly idea of how to take notes from a variety of sources and combine them into one paper.

While note taking can be overwhelming, it is important for teachers to help students learn that note taking is basically a matter of paraphrasing and writing down major points and supporting details. There are a number of note-taking strategies that students can implement; however, the use of note cards, where students limit the writing on cards to information about one topic at a time and from one source at a time, can be a valuable tool in helping students organize information. After notes are taken, the next step is to have students develop their narrative. Students should be aware that this is where they write out the information they have gathered and ask for the assistance of their peers in preparing the next revision of their work.

A question that arises is how to go about having students complete peer evaluations. The first step is to model for students. Even elementary students have had experiences where their work has been evaluated by a teacher, so we need to model how we go about completing an evaluation. As a part of peer evaluations of written work, it is important that the students understand that the purpose is to help them develop better written communication skills. It is equally important that there be interaction during and following the evaluation process. An informal setting that encourages interaction is best. For example, in one third grade class I had the

FIGURE 4-7 What the Students Want to Know about Their Topic

K (Know)	W (Want to know)	L (Learned)
had ceremonies

ate berries

lived in America | Did they have spiritual beliefs?

What other kinds or types of food did they eat?

Where did they live in America? | |

FIGURE 4-8 What the Students Have Learned Following Their Investigation

K (Know)	W (Want to know)	L (Learned)
had ceremonies ate berries lived in America	Did they have spiritual beliefs? What other kinds or types of food did they eat? Where did they live in America?	They had a well planned belief system. They used many kinds of tools and cooked many foods. There were many different tribes in America.

opportunity to work with, during this stage, if you had been a visitor in our room, you would have observed students in pairs and small groups, seated and scattered at tables and on the floor, busily marking away on papers with the dreaded red pen. Why the use of the red pen? Why not? Yes, we often suffer from the "red pen syndrome," but why not help our students at the elementary and middle school levels to overcome their fear and realize it is just another color of ink? This can be done using non-threatening peer-suggested revising and editing.

The key word is *nonthreatening.* There are a number of techniques that may be used to lead students through making corrections. One is the dot method in which a single dot (•) is placed in the margin by every line where a mechanical or grammatical error or question may be found. (Sometimes a check mark is preferred.) My experience is that this technique is more useful for those students who have had a number of opportunities to write—otherwise you have line after line of red dots!

A second suggestion is the use of a checklist or form on which comments are made. (See Figure 4-9.) This provides students with general

FIGURE 4-9 Editing Checklist

Author: _____

Title: _____

Date: _____

Peer editor: _____

Does it make sense?   Why or why not?

Spelling:

Punctuation:
(periods, question marks, commas, exclamation marks, quotation marks, etc.)

Paragraphs:

Capitals:

Excess words:

Strengths:

Weaknesses:

feedback and encourages a great deal of self-evaluation on the part of the writer.

Both techniques have positive aspects, so the teacher could use a combination of the two strategies mentioned (or others that you may find appropriate for the students you are working with). The purpose of revision and editing is to help students develop the best report or project possible. The focus should remain on using mechanics to help readers understand the content.

Peer work may be confined to students in the same grade level, but taking advantage of multi–grade-level peer evaluation can be useful. Students who have had a number of opportunities to write will be able to provide a host of recommendations for those less-experienced (i.e., younger, lower grade level) students. For example, a group of fifth graders at a middle school were adopted by a senior high English grammar class—a wonderful experience for all.

Of course, the ultimate goal is to develop a well-written, meaningful, organized report. But of what use is this to students if there is not some means to share? Sharing is a vital part of the writing process.

In social studies, the sharing stage of a written report may be implemented in a variety of ways. One suggestion is to move from having a written report to an oral report. In doing this, the student who wrote the report will present his findings by using strategies suggested earlier.

Another way for students to share their written work is by display on a bulletin board. This is most appropriate for brief reports (not longer than one or two pages). In using this strategy, it is important that all students in the class be guided to read and use the bulletin board so that true effective sharing can take place.

Another suggestion is the development of a class book for written reports. To form a book, place all student reports of a particular area of study in a folder for use by the class. The report book may be placed in the school library or media center for use by other groups of students.

ACTIVITIES

ACTIVITIES RELATED TO WRITTEN REPORTS

Making Soap (. . . Or Just About Anything)

Time Allotment: One or two class periods

Materials: Reference books, paper, pens, pencils, markers, posterboard, butcher or chart paper

Grade Level: Elementary and middle school

Making Soap (. . . Or Just About Anything) **continued**

Procedure: Students may write directions for doing something, such as making soap or some food dish, operating a machine, or reading a given graph or chart. Variation: For some topics, after the presentation the rest of the class may try out the directions for accuracy.

Captions Help Develop Understanding

Time Allotment: Varied

Materials: Magazines, photographs, glue, scissors, paper for mounting (chart or butcher paper), pens, pencils, markers

Grade Level: Elementary and middle school

Procedure: Students should look through appropriate magazines to find pictures related to the topic of study. They should cut out and mount the pictures. Finally, students should write captions for the pictures to help the viewer or reader understand more about the topic and pictures.

Create a "News" Story

Time Allotment: Two or three class periods

Materials: Reference materials, paper, pens, pencils

Grade Level: Elementary and middle school

Procedure: After studying the information given in newspaper articles (who, what, when, where, and why), students may identify a particular historical event and write a report as it might have appeared in the local newspaper.

Dear Diary

Time Allotment: Varied

Materials: Reference materials, paper, pencils, pens, construction paper, stapler

Grade Level: Elementary and middle school

Procedure: While completing a study on particular explorers, students may write entries in a diary that might have been kept by the explorer. Creative license may be used to embellish the entries, but factual information should be accurate and consistent. Students may later compare their entries with others for likenesses and differences.

Writer, Producer, Director

Time Allotment: Varied

Materials: Reference materials, paper, pens, pencils, cassete recorder and player

Writer, Producer, Director **continued**

Grade Level: Elementary and middle school

Procedure: Students may write a script for a tape-recorded program on a particular topic. Students may also complete the actual production of the script. Variation: In small groups, students may write original skits and later perform the skits for the rest of the class or other groups of students.

After Our Experience

Time Allotment: One or two class periods

Materials: Paper, pens, pencils, pictures, slides, any other appropriate materials

Grade Level: Elementary and middle school

Procedure: After a field trip or after investigating a certain event, students may develop a written explanation of the experience. Any supporting graphic aids that might help in their explanation should be included in their reports.

Develop a Travel Brochure

Time Allotment: Varied

Materials: Reference books, magazines, travel brochures, scissors, glue, pens, pencils, markers, crayons, white paper, construction paper

Grade Level: Elementary and middle school

Procedure: After studying about a particular place, students may develop a travel brochure. They may need to look at some examples of travel brochures in order to learn the types of information they should include. The information included in the student-developed brochures should be accurate as well as inviting. Variation: Students may also develop brochures for places of historic significance or for places important at certain dates in history (e.g., California during the gold rush).

I Want To Know

Time Allotment: Varied

Materials: Reference materials, textbooks, paper, pencils, pens

Grade Level: Elementary and middle school

Procedure: A valuable learning activity is for students to develop study guides. Small groups may locate sources of specific information. Later the groups may exchange guides and research other topics.

The following guidelines can help students develop a study guide.

I Want To Know **continued**

1. What is the topic being studied?
2. What questions or major facts should be studied?
3. What materials are needed for finding the information?
4. Will all group members answer all questions or one question per group member?
5. If there is disagreement, reread and find out the correct information.

What Might Have Happened

Time Allotment: One or two class periods

Materials: Reference materials, completed research reports, paper, pencils, pens

Grade Level: Elementary and middle school

Procedure: After students have completed research on a variety of topics, they may add another section to their reports in which they discuss how outcomes could have been changed if factors had been different. For example, how could the relocation of Native Americans have been avoided or handled differently than the Trail of Tears?

LISTENING

Listening may be defined as a "highly complex and interactive process in which spoken language is converted to meaning in the mind" (Lundsteen, 1989). According to Pflaumer (1971), ideal listeners are those who "keep an open, curious mind. They listen for new ideas everywhere, integrating what they hear with what they already know. They also know how to evaluate many points of view."

In the school setting, students are expected to listen for more than 50% of the school day (Lemlech, 1990). According to Burley-Allen (1982), students often graduate from high school having had less than six hours of instruction in methods or techniques for improving listening skills. Beyond the physical complexities that often interfere with active listening on the part of students, there are other reasons students may not be involved in active listening, including noise pollution in our society and lack of interaction in the classroom. One major reason is that students may choose not to listen (Moffet & Wagner, 1983; Lundsteen, 1989). Because of this, it is important that we take steps to find out if students are really listening.

First, we should understand that there are five goals for listening. These are (1) to distinguish sounds; (2) to understand messages; (3) to assist speakers and dismantle problems; (4) to comprehend and evaluate what is said; and (5) to enjoy, appreciate, and respond emotionally

(Wolven & Coakley, 1979). Although these seem logical, the fact that we tend to listen according to our own perceived needs or purposes explains why students tend only to half-listen, choosing to hear only what they believe is important to them. This, of course, is further complicated by the fact that listeners understand more rapidly than people speak (Block, 1993), which means most listeners are only partially involved in understanding or comprehending what they hear.

With this in mind there are steps that must be taken to encourage listening on the part of students. In the school setting, it is important that the teacher serve as a positive role model. This, of course, means actively listening not only during reports in a given classroom but during whole class or small group discussion, assembly programs, guest speakers, and any other time you would expect students to listen. When students are speaking, be sure that you are being attentive by providing eye contact and other response techniques (e.g., nodding, smiling, expressions) so that they will know you value their remarks and what they have to say is important. In addition, it is equally important that you monitor student listening and encourage more understanding between students concerning areas of interest, specialty, or needs by encouraging them to become better active listeners.

There are a number of reasons listening is so important in the area of social studies. First, the title itself implies interaction, that is, the *social* aspect of social studies. In order for true interaction to take place, at least one person must be involved in receiving a message of some sort. Among several means for communication, the one most commonly used in the average classroom setting is speaking and listening. In order to be effective participants in active listening, it is important that students become aware of how to listen.

One part of being aware of how to listen is to be able to identify factors that may interfere with listening. One factor is the classroom environment. The noise level within the classroom as well as outside noises (e.g., hall, playground, traffic, train) can lead to less than full attention. The temperature of the classroom also plays a part in how well students can accomplish listening tasks. If the room is too warm, the students may be uncomfortable, or, especially in the winter months, tend to fall asleep. The comfort level and seating arrangement also need to be considered according to the age, ability levels, and maturity levels of the students. A fourth factor to be considered is the type of presentation. Some types of presentations are more conducive to active listening than others given the factors mentioned so far and the needs of a particular group of students. Finally, the emotional and social factors of the classroom influence the listener. A nonthreatening and supportive atmosphere is conducive to all aspects related to learning, especially in areas where students may be asked to contribute.

ACTIVITIES

ACTIVITIES RELATED TO LISTENING
Does It All Make Sense

Time Allotment: One class period

Materials: Short story with erroneous or illogical sentences inserted

Grade Level: Elementary and middle school

Procedure: Select a story that relates to information being studied in social studies. Rewrite the story to include erroneous information or illogical sentences. Read the story to the students. The students should identify the sentences by using a predetermined signal such as raising their hand or standing.

"Listen My Children . . ."

Time Allotment: One class period

Materials: Appropriate short story or poem, questions

Grade Level: Elementary

Procedure: First have the students seated in a comfortable way (e.g., chairs, on carpet squares, padded floor, bean bag chairs). Explain to the students that you are going to read a story or poem related to what they have been studying in social studies. They should listen carefully so that they can discuss the main idea.

The Importance of Mood

Time Allotment: Varied

Materials: Prerecorded speeches on various topics

Grade Level: Upper elementary and middle school

Procedure: Students should listen to various speakers. From the tone used by the speakers, students should identify the mood of the speaker; that is, angry, apologetic, hysterical, happy, and so on.

Political Speeches

Time Allotment: Varied

Materials: Prerecorded political speeches

Grade Level: Upper elementary and middle school

Procedure: Students should listen to a political speech. The students should then point out any uses of appeals to emotion, or other means politicians may use to get votes.

continued

And Then

Time Allotment: Varied

Materials: Short paragraphs with complete messages

Grade Level: Elementary

Procedure: Read short paragraphs. Have the students write what they think would happen next and why. After students have an opportunity to share the new endings, they should listen to the rest of the paragraph and compare their thoughts with those of the author.

Communication

Time Allotment: One or two class periods

Materials: Morse code on duplicated sheets for students, two or more class-made telegraph sets, paper, pencils

Grade Level: Elementary and middle school

Procedure: First discuss methods of communication. (Topics may include telephone, computer, radio, television, etc.) One method of communication is the telegraph. This was especially important in the history of our country.

After the discussion about the history and importance of the telegraph, show a chart of the Morse code and demonstrate for the students. You may also demonstrate how messages may be tapped out using a pencil on a desk, for the purpose of this lesson.

The students should work in pairs. Each student should write a short message (10 words) and send the message to their partner. Then the partner will reply.

Focus on listening for accuracy.

CBs and Walkie-Talkies

Time Allotment: Varied

Materials: Poster board or chart paper, markers, pens, pencils, paper, CB radio (if possible), set of walkie-talkies, police scanner

Grade Level: Elementary

Procedure: After a discussion about communication, ask students if they are familiar with the use of CB radios. Mention to them how various code words or terms are often used by people when using CBs. Make and present a chart showing some of the familiar terms and codes. (See Table 4-3.)

Also discuss with students the importance of codes used by policemen. You might include in this discussion why codes are used and the importance of accuracy by the dispatcher as well as the officers in the field. If possible, give the students an opportunity to listen to a police scanner.

CBs and Walkie-Talkies **continued**

TABLE 4-3 CB Codes and Terms

Code	Meaning
10-1	Receiving poorly
10-2	Receiving well
10-3	Stop transmitting
10-4	OK, message received
10-6	Busy, stand by
10-7	Out of service, leaving air
10-9	Repeat message
10-11	Talking too fast
10-16	Make pickup at _____
10-17	Urgent business
10-23	Stand by
10-36	Correct time is _____
10-42	Traffic accident at _____
10-46	Assist motorist
10-65	Awaiting your next message

Finally, students are probably most familiar with walkie-talkies. These are often used in schools and larger stores or malls for communication. If possible, students should have the opportunity to communicate using walkie-talkies.

Variation: Students may develop their own set of codes and terms and then practice using these in their communication.

Sales Pitch

Time Allotment: Varied

Materials: Taped radio advertisements

Grade Level: Elementary and middle school

Procedure: Record some radio advertisements. Students should listen to these and analyze how the advertisers try to get people to buy or use their products.

Mrs. Jones Has Green Cabbage (Mr. Jones Has a Log Cabin)

Time Allotment: One class period

Materials: One or two short statements on slips of paper

Grade Level: Elementary and middle school

Procedure: The old game of "gossip" can help students learn or reinforce the importance of listening carefully.

Mrs. Jones Has Green Cabbage (Mr. Jones Has a Log Cabin) **continued**

> First select a student to start the gossip. The student should whisper a message to the next student and so on until the message has been given to all the students. The last student should say the statement loud enough for the class to hear. Compare the beginning and ending messages. Repeat with a new message.
>
> ## Do What?
>
> | | |
> |---:|:---|
> | **Time Allotment:** | One or two class periods |
> | **Materials:** | Sets of written directions to be read |
> | **Grade Level:** | Elementary |
> | **Procedure:** | Depending on the age of the students, give a series of directions for |
>
> them to follow. For example, with younger students you might say, "Go to the door, turn in circles two times, and hop back to your seat." For older students you might say, "Hop to the closet, open the door, look in the brown box, find a red toy truck, put it on the second shelf from the bottom, stretch your arms, and return to your seat." The rest of the group must listen carefully to know if directions are followed correctly.

HELPFUL HINTS FOR UNIT 4:

1. Describe how language arts was included in social studies when you were a student. How would you want to include language arts in social studies as a teacher?
2. Develop a file of social studies trade books you feel would be appropriate for a variety of grade levels. (Information on at least ten books should be included for a starter file.) Develop an activity to reinforce the information or motivate the student to read each book.
3. According to one study, students spend about half the school day listening. What can you do to help them improve their listening skills, especially in social studies activities?
4. Develop a semantic map for a familiar historical event. What questions would you use to help students get started with their maps on this topic?
5. Write a brief report on some topic of special interest. Read the report on tape. Evaluate the tape for your use of expression and voice modulation.
6. With a particular group of students in mind, develop a simulation of a current affair that may be of interest to the students (this may include issues of local or national interest).

REFERENCES

Atwell, N. (Ed.). (1990). *Coming to know: Writing to learn in the intermediate grades.* Portsmouth, NH: Heinemann.

Block, C. (1993). *Teaching the language arts: Expanding thinking through student-centered instruction.* Boston: Allyn & Bacon.

Brozo, W. G. & Tomlinson, C. M. (1986, December). Literature: The key to lively content courses. *The Reading Teacher, 40,* 288–293.

Burley-Allen, M. (1982). *Listening: The forgotten skills.* New York: Wiley.

Burns, P., Roe, B., & Ross, E. P. (1992). *Teaching reading in today's elementary schools.* Boston: Houghton-Mifflin.

Calkins, L. M. (1986). *The art of teaching writing.* Portsmouth, NH: Heinemann.

Collins, C. (1992). *126 strategies that build the language arts.* Boston: Allyn & Bacon.

Jarolimek, J. & Parker, W. C. (1993). *Social studies in elementary education* (9th ed.). New York: Macmillan.

Lemlech, J. K. (1990). *Curriculum and instructional methods for the elementary school* (2nd ed.). New York: Macmillan.

Loban, W. (1976). *Language development: Kindergarten through grade twelve.* Urbana, IL: National Council of Teachers of English.

Lundsteen, S. (1989). *Language arts: A problem solving approach.* New York: Harper & Row.

McClure, J. (1989). *Teaching poetry.* Portsmouth, NH: Heinemann.

Michaelis, J. U. (1992). *Social studies for children: A guide to basic instruction* (10th ed.). Needham Heights, MA: Allyn & Bacon. .

Moffet, J. & Wagner, B. J. (1983). *Student-centered language arts and reading, K-13: A handbook for teachers* (3rd ed.). Boston: Houghton-Mifflin.

"Notable 1990 Children's Trade Books in the Field of Social Studies." (1991, April/May). *Social Education, 55,* 253–260.

Ogle, D. M. (1986). KWL: A teaching model that develops active reading of expository text. *The Reading Teacher, 39,* 64–70.

Pflaumer, E. M. (1971). A definition of listening. In C. Diker (Ed.), *Listening: Readings.* Metuchen, NJ: Scarecrow Press.

Sampson, M. R. (1986). *The pursuit of literacy: Early reading and writing.* Dubuque, IA: Kendall/Hunt.

Storey, D. C. (1982, April). Reading in the content areas: Fictionalized biographies and diaries for social studies. *The Reading Teacher, 35,* 796–798.

Wolven, A. D. & Coakley, C. J. (1979). Listening instructions (TRIP Booklet). Urbana, IL: ERIC Clearinghouse on Reading and Communication Association.

Zarnowski, M. (1988, November). Learning about fictionalized biographies: A reading and writing approach. *The Reading Teacher, 42,* 136–142.

STUDY QUESTIONS FOR UNIT 5: **1.** What are some of the factors influencing inclusion of religion in social studies? **2.** What is the most prevalent reason given for not including religion in social studies instruction? **3.** Describe a major reason for including religion as a part of cultural studies. **4.** Explain why educators should be knowledgeable about diverse cultures and religions.

INTRODUCTION As described in Unit 1, social studies may be defined as the study of the past, present, and prospects for the future; the study of the social and life skills needed to become productive citizens in a chang-

Religion and Social Studies

ing world, including the knowledge needed by global citizens. Based on this definition we, as teachers, often tend to focus on specific historical and cultural aspects and provide for our students a somewhat less than accurate representation of our society. That is, we look at specific events on the historical timeline of our society and from that timeline select specific cultural influences to highlight. Unfortunately, by doing this, we fail to provide our students with full understanding of the past of our society, and more importantly, we are not preparing our students to be productive global citizens in the future.

Although the historical information we provide for students is normally based on those events that have traditionally been most important in our society (i.e., discoverers, pioneers, presidents, wars, expansion), the cultural information traditionally provided for students may no longer be adequate. Given the innovations in technology and travel that make our society a more global society, our students are more likely to deal with diverse cultures on a regular basis in the future. In looking at how to deal with cultures, it is important for students at the elementary and middle school levels first to become familiar with those that are representative of our country and then to expand.

Many elementary and middle school social studies teachers have been faithful in following the guidelines prepared by a number of organizations and textbook publishers concerning the types and amount of cultural information to introduce to students. We tend, however, to avoid controversial issues of cultural significance, especially when touching on the area of religion. There are a number of valid reasons why educators avoid the area of religion, but it is important that we, as educators, understand the role of religion in the public school curriculum from a historical, legal, current, and futuristic perspective.

HISTORICAL PERSPECTIVE

Religion has been a significant factor in the area of education, especially in the United States, from the foundation of our country. Religious events and commitments have influenced history as well as culture. Students cannot fully understand the successful results of the long campaign against slavery without learning about the role Christian abolitionists played. Without understanding the role of African American churches in the years following the Civil War in the South, the history of the vibrant Black culture is lost (Matthews, 1979). In addition, in more recent history the importance of the religious convictions of the late Dr. Martin Luther King, Jr., which were shared not only by African American Christians but by white Protestant, Catholic, and Jewish believers, led to a number of changes in the culture of the United States in the areas of civil rights and equality.

In terms of curriculum, religion has again been a major area of importance. The early colonies continued the European pattern of schools being under the auspices or direction of established religious organizations. Materials developed and used as a part of daily instruction had a religious focus, primarily related to the values and morals advocated by the Christian belief system. Examples that may be noted include the Horn Book and the New England Primer. The use of the Bible and other religious materials continued for a long period of time, even after the development of tax-supported public schools.

Thomas Jefferson and James Madison were key influences in the development of the concept of free, tax-supported schools (Reichley, 1985), yet their belief system maintained that Biblical instruction was a natural part of the curriculum. The Common School movement and the influence of Horace Mann on the limitations of religious-related instruction was significant in raising the level of controversy concerning religion as a part of the public school curriculum.

Because of the nonsectarian limitations advocated by Mann, the religious instruction was primarily related to Protestantism, therefore leading to the development or reopening of a number of church-related schools, including those under the direction of the Catholic Church (Shafer, 1990). In addition, with the increasing numbers of immigrants in the 19th century, along with the population growth of the cities, the emphasis on limited religious instruction being provided in public schools was a point of contention, and the argument for separation of church and state became more evident. With societal changes, such as the Progressive Era and New Deal, and the mind-set of the general population following World War I, religion was once again at the forefront of public education.

In a number of public school systems throughout the United States, "released-time" programs were instituted (Reichley, 1985). In such situations, students were given released time during the school day for religious instruction from the private sector. This continued as a method until mid-century, when the societal focus changed to more recognition of individual rights and the rights guaranteed by the laws of the United States.

LEGAL PERSPECTIVE

The legal perspective of religion as a part of the school curriculum has changed and will probably continue to do so. In our culturally diverse society, religion is commonly accepted as a private matter. This view has developed over a number of years and, as a result of a number of legal battles, has led to the present views regarding the inclusion or absence of religion as a topic of study in the cultural realm of the social studies curriculum.

The relationship between public schools and religion has been the focus of a number of constitutional issues and clarifications or rulings by a number of courts, most significant being the United States Supreme Court. The First Amendment of the United States Constitution begins, "Congress shall make no law respecting an establishment of religion, or prohibiting the free exercise thereof." One of the first cases that focused on the First Amendment was *Pierce v. Society of Sisters* in 1925. This particular decision regarded an Oregon law which *required* students to attend public schools rather than church-sponsored private schools. In 1947, an extremely important decision regarding the preference of one religion over another was brought into focus by the decision handed down as a result of *Everson v. Board of Education*. This eliminated the teaching of religious thought and doctrine in public school facilities in released-time programs; however, in 1952, the decision as a result of *Zorach v. Clausen* made a point of saying that students could be excused from public school attendance in order to receive religious instruction (Stokes and Pfeffer, 1962).

With the movement in the 1960s toward attention to civil and individual rights of expression, the Supreme Court handed down the *Abington v. Shemp* (1963) decision. This decision banned school-sponsored morning devotions of Bible reading and prayer.

Since the landmark decision in 1963, two cases that have provoked a great deal of controversy are *Wallace v. Jaffree* (1985) and *Edwards v. Aguillard* (1987). In these decisions, the Supreme Court mandated that laws requiring moments of silence and the teaching of alternative theories of the origin of humans were unconstitutional, as they promoted religious doctrine.

The general guidelines for instruction concerning religion that are still used today were established by the decision in *Lemon v. Kurtzman* (1971). Often referred to as the "Lemon test," the questions that must be answered are:

1. Does the school's action have a secular or nonsecular purpose? and
2. Is the primary purpose of the instruction to advance religion?
    (Pitts, 1991)

Educators need to ask themselves if they are inculcating religious devotion or exploring religion for its historical and cultural importance.

As we continue to see changes in society, there will surely be changes concerning the role of religion in the school curriculum. Tax credits for parents or guardians of students who attend private schools, the role of government (federal, state, and local) in the development of programs in private and church-sponsored schools, and the reforming of public schools regarding cultural information in the curriculum to reflect a more diverse society are issues to be considered.

CURRENT AND FUTURE PERSPECTIVE

The basic purpose of the public school social studies curriculum has been to encourage development of qualities needed by citizens and the development of skills related to the content. Although it has been noted that the development of citizens in our current society and for the future will require a broader and more thorough understanding of cultural likenesses and differences, little attention is given to the religious aspects of culture.

There are a number of valid reasons for the lack of instruction related to religion, but the matter of controversy seems to be most prevalent. First, most Americans consider religious beliefs to be a very private matter. Because of this, the view has been that it is the responsibility of the family and religious institutions to teach religious doctrine to students. However, because this practice often provides a narrow margin of information (i.e., only teaching about their own religious belief system), and the fact that there is a growing population for whom organized religion is not a part of family life, the role of wider instruction *about* religion may need to be addressed through instruction in the public school arena. The goal, of course, is to increase understanding about religion from a cultural perspective (Chmelynski, 1991).

Recent trends in available materials have included cultural information regarding religion, but because the information may be somewhat limited the criticism used previously concerning textbooks has been made. That is, materials give favored status to certain religions (ASCD, 1987) and are not equal in the types or amount of information provided.

Another reason for the avoidance of religion in social studies is that the school community may have concerns about the inclusion of religion. In many settings, the role of the community takes precedence over how or if a specific topic of study will be addressed. This is especially true for study concerning religion in our society. Some schools represent the diversity of our society, but others are largely representative of one cultural group. If the community leaders oppose the instruction and the

TABLE 5-1 Videos that May be Used In Relation to Religion

Video	Source
The Greek Myths: Myth as Science, Religion and Drama	Encyclopedia Britannica Educational Corporation
Faith & Belief: Five Major World Religions	Knowledge Unlimited
Culture: What Is It?	Knowledge Unlimited
The Arab World	Knowledge Unlimited
Israel—Yesterday and Today	Knowledge Unlimited
Daily Life in the Ancient World	Knowledge Unlimited
A Nation of Immigrants	Guidance Associates
Rebuilding the American Nation (1865–1890)	Guidance Associates
The Constitution: Foundation of Our Government	Guidance Associates

participation of their children concerning religious influences in cultures different from their own, it may prove so controversial that teachers decide to leave out instruction.

Community leaders who have developed and perpetuated certain beliefs about diverse cultures may feel threatened by the influx of information concerning culture, especially information related to religion. Although we as parents and educators agree that children form their opinions of others at a very early age, it is also important to remember that we are responsible for helping them develop those opinions. If we present closed or possibly biased views, then we are not accurately presenting other cultures to our children. In addition, for upper elementary and middle school students, who are at the brink of establishing their own perceptions, it is equally important that we provide techniques they may use in order to check for bias or stereotypical views. If we leave out portions of information about cultures, we are not preparing our students for the future, but placing the limitations of the past on their outlook.

SUGGESTIONS REGARDING RELIGION IN THE CURRICULUM

As the citizens of the future, our students must be prepared to communicate and display some level of understanding of diverse cultures. In order to help them, we must first develop some level of understanding ourselves. One suggestion is that we, as educators, become more knowledgeable about the influence religion has in various cultures in order to make religion a natural part of social studies instruction. It is not feasible for us to discuss all religions, but it is important that we be familiar with

TABLE 5-2 Religious Groups Predominant in the United States

Baptist	Methodist
Church of Christ	Mormon
Episcopalian	Pentecostal
Jewish	Presbyterian
Lutheran	Roman Catholic

*Modified from Kosmin and Lachman, 1993.

NOTE: This list is in no way meant to be construed as representative of one geographical area. The predominant group will differ from community to community.

those most prominent on a national basis. The list in Table 5-2 is not comprehensive, but it provides some insight into the religions that may be most predominant in social studies instruction.

FIGURE 5-1 Geographical Representation of Major Religious Groups in the Continental United States

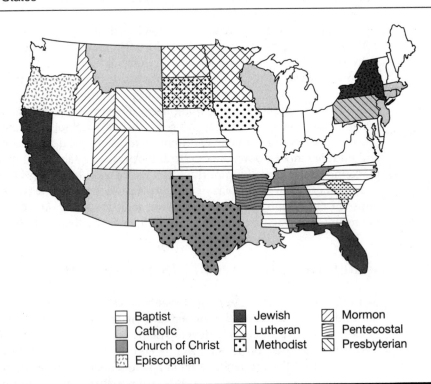

☐ Baptist	■ Jewish	◪ Mormon
☐ Catholic	⊠ Lutheran	▤ Pentecostal
■ Church of Christ	⊡ Methodist	◩ Presbyterian
▨ Episcopalian		

*Adapted from Kasmin and Lachman, 1993.

FIGURE 5-2 Hindu, Muslim, Christian, Jew?

HINDU, MUSLIM, CHRISTIAN, JEW?
by Gary Graham, 1990

How did it all happen, you Hindu, Muslim, Christian, Jew?
How can each one be right, with a different point of view?
How can we not see beyond the common breed and trend?
How did it all happen, you Hindu, Muslim, Christian, Jew?
How did personified worship pastel the original hue?
There is a higher power
On that you can rely.
But no one's certain about life
Until the day they die.

In addition, in thinking about religion as an area for instruction as a part of social studies, it is important that we look at the makeup of our own classes and schools. The influence of religion in culture is not limited to foreign culture, but can be found in any given classroom. For example, in an urban setting, the role of religion may be as important or more important for some students as the regular attendance of classes. This is equally true for many students in rural settings. Not only should educators become familiar with the major religious influence in their own school community, but the geographical region in which they work with students. In some areas of our country, there is greater variety of beliefs than in others.

Religion as a part of social studies instruction is extremely important. We must be willing to attempt to prepare our students as global citizens in a world that is ever shrinking because of advances in technology and travel. We must constantly be on guard not to promote our own values or beliefs, and it is equally important to provide our students with methods for doing the same, while accepting those of diverse beliefs.

Finally, educators need to use professional judgement. As with any topic of controversy, find out about school policy long before beginning instruction. If the local school or school system does not have a policy, one needs to be developed. If there is no threat of litigation, the educator as well as the students will enjoy instruction to a greater extent.

TABLE 5-3 Suggestions for Including Religion In the Curriculum

1. Educators and the school community must be committed to the belief that the study of religion is important for students.
2. Educators (teachers and administrators) must be honest with themselves and the school community regarding the types of information taught about religion within the school.
3. Educators must be objectively informed about different religions. They need to be able to help students learn how religions are a part of cultures.
4. Educators must be committed to the exclusion of their own religious beliefs and practices from instruction.

Even after a policy is in place, it is important that instruction about religion be monitored. Teaching as though a representative of each religious group mentioned in the course of study is inside the classroom will encourage a more positive atmosphere and encourage the students' respect of various cultural expressions of religion. The focus is to help develop better long-term understanding by students, and this can only take place through careful, thoughtful instruction that leads students to think for themselves.

ACTIVITIES

ACTIVITIES RELATED TO THE STUDY OF RELIGION IN SOCIAL STUDIES

Findings From Fables

Time Allotment: Four or five class periods

Materials: A number of copies of fables, materials for costumes and props

Grade Level: Elementary and middle school

Procedure: Discuss how fables are part of all cultures and how they provide guidance or reasoning for behavior. Help students become familiar with several well-known fables. In groups of four or five, have students write and present a skit illustrating an application of the message of the fable as it relates to present day. Discuss with students how the fables presented could be similar in various cultures. Show examples.

Problems with Prejudging

Time Allotment: Two to four class periods

Materials: Pictures of food or actual foods, paper cups, plastic utensils, paper towels

Grade Level: Elementary and middle school

Procedure: Write the definition of prejudge on the board or overhead. Ask students to name one food they have prejudged before tasting it. List the foods on the board. Ask students to describe the basis for their opinion (color, cooking or serving method). Ask students to tell if they later changed their mind about the food, and if so, why?

Perception

Time Allotment: One class period

Materials: Stories to be read to class with pictures or illustrations appropriate for the activity

Grade Level: Lower elementary and elementary

Procedure: Discuss with students how people often imagine how a person might look from what they know or have heard about that person. Tell or read them a story about a person. After the story, ask the students to draw or describe the person. Finally, show students a picture or drawing of the person.

Students should make a comparison about what they thought and what was reality.

Plans for the Holidays

Time Allotment: One or two class periods

Materials: Appropriate story for activity and level of students, board or overhead

Grade Level: Lower elementary

Procedure: Ask students to develop a list of things that families often do to prepare for Christmas. Read *An Island Christmas* by Lyn Joseph (Clarion, 1992) or some other appropriate book to the class. Following the story, enlist the help of students in listing the preparations the family in the story makes. Help students compare the two lists, noting similarities and differences.

Stereotypes

Time Allotment: One class period

Materials: Board, chart, markers

Grade Level: Upper elementary and middle school

Procedure: Students should define stereotype. List definitions on the board. In small groups or as a whole group, students should discuss their definitions. Questions the teacher may use to stimulate thought and discussion could include:

Stereotypes **continued**

1. Why do you think stereotypes exist?
2. How are stereotypes destroyed?
3. Do we have stereotypes about cultures different from our own?

   Stereotypes of various religious groups:

   ▮ Jews are stingy
   ▮ Catholics are all in the mob
   ▮ African American churches do nothing but yell and dance during their services
   ▮ Amish are dumb because they do not fight back
   ▮ Hindus believe that their ancestors may be cows

Remembering the Renowned

Time Allotment: Three or four class periods

Materials: Biographies of famous people (appropriate reading levels), chart, timer

Grade Level: Upper elementary and middle school

Procedure: Have students list the names of as many famous people, living or dead, as they can think of in five minutes. On the board, or overhead, make a list of what made each person famous.

Explain to the students that in the next few days they will be reading about famous people. Three questions should be completed about each person. These are:

1. What did you like most about the person?
2. What made this person outstanding compared to others?
3. What did the person do to become famous?

The students should be prepared to share their findings with the rest of the class.

Rite of Passage

Time Allotment: Three or four class periods

Materials: Appropriate books from libraries, appropriate videos, video player, chart paper, markers

Grade Level: Middle school

Procedure: Every culture has its own way of establishing when a person becomes an adult, or at least when they are expected to take on additional responsibilities. Often this rite of passage is part of the belief system traditionally accepted by a particular religious group. In this activity, the students investigate various cultural beliefs, origin of belief, and so forth.

In order to get students started, a film or video of a particular rite might be shown, for example the procedures followed during a Bar Mitzvah.

HELPFUL HINTS FOR UNIT 5:

1. In looking back at your school experiences, what do you remember about religion as a part of social studies? How do you want your students to remember religion as a part of social studies?
2. Develop a list of religions that you feel you need to become more familiar with in order to provide your students with more accurate information.
3. Some professionals feel that the use of plays or skits do not accurately present cultural information to students, especially as related to religion and culture. Give specific examples of religious ceremonies that may be presented in plays or skits. Give your opinion of the usefulness of each as a means of developing understanding by students.
4. Visit the local curriculum or teachers resource center. Locate and review any commercial materials that may be of help in providing instruction for students in relation to religion as a part of culture.

REFERENCES

Abington v. Shemp, 374 U.S. 203 (1963).

Association for Supervision and Curriculum Development. (1987). *Religion in the Curriculum* (A Report from the ASCD Panel on Religion in the Curriculum). Alexandria, VA: Author.

Chmelynski, C. (1991). Religion Makes a Comeback in the Classroom. *School Board News, 22,* 8.

Edwards v. Aguillard, 55 L.W. 4860 (No. 85-1513) (U.S. June 19, 1987).

Everson v. Board of Education, 330, U.S. 1 (1947).

Graham, G. (1990). *Contemporary Christian Composition.* Unpublished manuscript.

Kosmin, B. A. & Lachman, S. P. (1993). *One nation under God: Religion in contemporary American society.* New York: Harmony Books.

Lemon v. Kurtzman, 403 U.S. 602 (1971).

Matthews, D. G. (1979). *Religion in the Old South.* Chicago: University of Chicago Press.

Pierce v. Society of Sisters, 268, U.S. 518 (1925).

Pitts, M. E. (1991). A closer look: Religion and public education. In A. Ellis, J. Fouts, & A. Glenn (Eds.), *Teaching and learning secondary social studies.* New York: Harper Collins.

Reichley, A. J. (1985). *Religion in American public life.* Washington: Brookings Institution.

Shafer, M. L. (1990). Public schools and religion. In I. Cully & K. B. Cully (Eds.), *Harper's encyclopedia of religious education* (pp. 526–527). San Francisco: Harper & Row.

Stokes, A. P. & Pfeffer, L. (1963). *Church and state in the United States.* New York: Harper & Row.

Wallace v. Jaffree, 472, U.S. 38 (1985).

Zorach v. Clausen, 343, U.S. 306 (1952).

UNIT 6

STUDY QUESTIONS FOR UNIT 6: **1.** Why is a discussion of American heritage important as a part of social studies? **2.** What is your definition of multicultural education? **3.** Why is ongoing multicultural education important for elementary and middle school students? **4.** "Activity-based lessons are important as a part of multicultural education." Is this statement true? Why or why not? **5.** What major cultural groups do we need to include in our ongoing cultural experience?

INTRODUCTION Who are we? Where did we come from? What makes us who we are? It is impossible for

American Heritage

us to presume we can answer these questions adequately for every individual student we meet, but it is important that we help our students learn about the makeup of our society, from a historical, current, and futuristic perspective.

National thinking has changed in many respects since the settlement of Jamestown in 1607. Historically, we can note the controversy and the shaping of the thinking that led to the Revolutionary War and the establishment of the United States of America. In addition from a historical perspective, we can trace the evolution of thinking that led to the freeing of slaves and movement of many Native Americans from one geographical area to another, as well as the many reasons for large numbers of immigrants coming to the United States over a period of time.

The discussion of American heritage should include a look at a number of the major groups of people who have traditionally been recognized as prominent in the makeup of the citizenry of the United States. Educators in schools spend more time with children than almost any other adults. We have the responsibility to help students become academically capable while they develop social awareness about themselves and the world around them. One step toward accomplishing this monumental task is to provide some level of multicultural education on a day-to-day basis.

In order to provide multicultural education, it is first necessary to define the term. Recently, I heard a teacher give a definition of multicultural education as learning how others think and live outside the classroom. It seems to me that this definition is pretty accurate, but the definition of multicultural education varies depending on the group or individual using the term. Some definitions emerge from such disciplines as education, sociology, or anthropology. Other definitions are based on the views of certain professional organizations or agencies (Hernandez, 1989). While definitions vary, however, the basic premise is that multicultural education should provide "... an environment that recognizes differences among people, perceives cultural differences as strengths rather than weaknesses, and emphasizes the importance of differences in the educational process . . ." (Baruth & Manning, 1992).

Multicultural education should be an interdisciplinary approach within the total curriculum rather than a "polka and piñata" approach. Such approaches do not work because being aware of diversity does not necessarily result in acceptance and respect of individuals within the cultural group. In addition, well-meaning multicultural programs may serve only cosmetic purposes if students and school personnel harbor long-held cultural biases and stereotypes. To be effective, responsive programs recognize the need to both inform and change negative attitudes and long-held prejudices.

UNITED STATES: SALAD AND STEW

Early in this century, one purpose of the schools was to absorb children into the national culture. Children were required to speak and to write English throughout their school experience, with no focus or consideration given to their ethnic or cultural heritage. This was supposed to continue into the personal lives of the children so that English would become the predominent language used. The goal was for all persons in the United States to melt together to form a society where the people were alike, eliminating diverse groups. The term that was often used to describe the United States was "melting pot."

The term *melting pot* came from a play by Ira Zangwill which was popular in the early 1900s.

> America is God's crucible, the great Melting Pot where all races of Europe are melting and reforming! . . . The real American has not yet arrived. He is only in the Crucible, I tell you—he will be the fusion of all races, the coming superman. (Zangwill, 1909)

Today, where cultural differences are recognized as strengths and not weaknesses, the melting pot theory is no longer accepted. A new term, such as tossed salad or vegetable stew, which typifies the contributions of a number of groups to the national culture while giving emphasis to the individual groups, may be more accurate.

Our national culture is a combination of the influences of various groups, the result of many learning experiences that have been provided throughout history, and the hope of continuance into the future. For our students, it is an awareness that we cannot live separately but that we depend on one another.

In explaining what the national culture of the United States is all about, we must understand that although we may have important differences, those likenesses we share are the foundation of our national culture. For example, all people have the same basic needs of food, shelter, respect, and love (Lay-Dopyera & Dopyera, 1987). In addition, in our culture we have certain freedoms because of the government of our country.

Focus on the national culture should help students develop a sense of belonging. For students who have no strong connections with an ethnic heritage, this helps them to know that the national culture is important. For students who may have strong ties with another culture, this helps them to develop a sense of belonging.

By helping students understand that they may belong to more than one culture, we will help them to respect one another as individuals. This is a strong step in helping to dismantle and avoid the development of prejudices and stereotypical viewpoints.

ACTIVITIES

ACTIVITIES RELATED TO UNITED STATES: SALAD AND STEW
Why U.S.A.?

Time Allotment: One or two class periods

Materials: Reference materials, paper, pens, chart paper, markers

Grade Level: Elementary and middle school

Procedure: After a study of various groups that are important in the American heritage, ask students to brainstorm concerning the name of our country, as well as why it was named as it is or according to whom it could have been named. Record or have a student record responses on a chart. Next have students look in reference materials for additional information to support the other names.

The President

Time Allotment: One or two class periods

Materials: Reference materials, paper, pens

Grade Level: Elementary and middle school

The President **continued**

Procedure: Students should investigate the following question:

What qualifications does the President of the United States need to have? The investigation should focus on citizenship requirements as well as a need for cultural understanding. Do the students feel the current qualifications are adequate for the present? future? Changes or modifications the students feel should be made should be expressed and justification given.

Made in America

Time Allotment: One or two class periods

Materials: Object brought in by students, bulletin board, push pins, markers, paper to make labels for objects

Grade Level: Elementary and middle school

Procedure: Have the students bring in objects that represent their day-to-day lives in the United States. Display the objects on a bulletin board. Examples: Levis labels, McDonald's bags, Coke cans.

This Is My Country

Time Allotment: One or two class periods

Materials: Large butcher paper, markers, crayons, reference materials, pens, writing paper

Grade Level: Elementary and middle school

Procedure: Using an opaque or overhead projector, trace or draw world maps on large pieces of butcher paper for each group of students. Each group should be responsible for coloring in an area from which major groups migrated to America. A short report should be developed by each group and attached to their display of the map.

How Do You Say "Hello"?

Time Allotment: One or two class periods

Materials: Chalk, chalkboard, chart paper, markers

Grade Level: Elementary

Procedure: To help students understand that a number of terms may be used to represent the same thing, ask students to name all the ways they might use to say hello (i.e., greet someone). Examples might include Hi, Howdy, Yo. Discuss the various terms and when they might be used. Students might also be asked to role-play various scenarios about the terms.

IRISH AMERICANS

The term Irish American often conjures up images developed through the media over time—the jolly policeman directing traffic or walking a beat, the Irish American priest, or merrymakers celebrating St. Patrick's Day. Americans of Irish descent can be included in each picture above, but it is important to note that they are also a part of everyday American national culture. In focusing on activities about Irish Americans there are a number of factors that should be included in the background knowledge of the educator guiding the study.

The immigration from Ireland began some time ago, therefore they are considered as "old" or "early" immigrants. This early immigration was primarily for economic and personal or religious reasons. The first Irish immigrants seemed to blend well with the British immigrants; however, they, like many other cultural groups, began early on to develop communities because of their shared beliefs, values, and customs.

Over the following generations, especially the third and fourth generations, assimilation of Irish Americans into the realm of the national culture has been significant. While this is generally true, it is important to note that the basic family values and belief in community goals are still a part of the everyday lifestyles of many Irish Americans (Feagin, 1978).

As educators, we need to be aware that although third, fourth, or even further removed generations may make up the student population we work with, ethnic behaviors and beliefs may still have a significant influence on how they perceive one another and how they view their role as citizens. It is important to learn and help our students learn about the cultural influences through activity-based studies.

ACTIVITIES

ACTIVITIES RELATED TO IRISH AMERICANS
Wars and What They Mean

Time Allotment: Two or three class periods

Materials: Reference materials, pens, paper

Grade Level: Middle school

Procedure: First discuss the history of Ireland and why some of the conflicts have occurred. Then discuss with students how this might have an effect on Irish Americans. Have students check in various reference materials to come up with answers.

continued

Famous Irish Americans—Then and Now

Time Allotment: Two or three class periods

Materials: Reference materials, chart or butcher paper, paper, pens, pencils, markers

Grade Level: Upper elementary and middle school

Procedure: After an introduction to the study of Irish Americans, have students identify famous Irish Americans in history or today's events. This may be extended to those of Irish American descent in the local community. Variation: Make a timeline and have students write a brief description of the person and when they were born and what made them famous.

The Old Immigrants

Time Allotment: Two or three class periods

Materials: Reference materials, pencils, paper, chart paper, markers

Grade Level: Upper elementary and middle school

Procedure: People from Ireland immigrated to the United States for a variety of reasons (e.g., economic, political, social). Irish immigrants were some of the first to come to the United States. Students should investigate the various reasons for immigration as well as the situations the immigrants encountered.

Brainstorming sessions should be considered to help the students get started with their investigation. Possibly divide the class into three (or more) groups and have charts made of the conclusions. (See the attached example.)

Immigration From Ireland

Reasons for Immigration	
Makeup of immigrants	
Problems encountered in trying to immigrate	
Where did they settle on arrival?	
Discrimination encountered	

continued

Irish American Heritage: More than St. Patrick's Day

Time Allotment: Flexible

Materials: Reference materials, resource speakers, chart paper, markers, pens, pencils, paper

Grade Level: Elementary and middle school

Procedure: Although St. Patrick's Day is probably the most widely recognized holiday or traditional day of celebration for Irish Americans, there are other cultural celebrations of equal importance. Using the background knowledge students have about St. Patrick's Day, branch off into further investigations. This would be an opportune activity to bring in local Irish American historians to help students gain a better understanding.

ITALIAN AMERICANS

The Italian American community has assimilated (third or fourth generations) into the national culture quite well. Attending public schools, participating in community activities, and working hand in hand with others outside the realm of the Italian American community are reflections of this assimilation.

It is important for educators to understand that although a great deal of assimilation has taken place, there are still factors that are unique for those citizens of primarily Italian American heritage. Some of these factors include a rich family life, strong community bonds with others of Italian American heritage, and celebrations of holidays in traditional ways.

Through activities that focus on a realistic look at contemporary and historic facts about Italian Americans it is hoped that students will develop an understanding and appreciation of the contributions of the Italian American community to the national culture.

ACTIVITIES

ACTIVITIES RELATED TO ITALIAN AMERICANS

Pasta: It's Not Just Spaghetti

Time Allotment: Flexible

Pasta: It's Not Just Spaghetti **continued**

Materials: Recipe for pasta, ingredients, work and cooking space, additional adult help, aprons, vacuum, reference materials

Grade Level: Elementary

Procedure: Have students brainstorm about Italian foods. One that will surely be named is spaghetti. Have students research different types of pasta and their uses. As a follow-up and interest-building activity, have students make pasta. As a variation, different types of pasta may be purchased and students may prepare a variety of dishes.
Variation: Students may investigate questions, such as whether certain types of pasta are more associated with one area of Italy than another.

NOTE: This same type of activity may be applied to other cultures. Helga Parnell has written a series of cultural cookbooks, for example *Cooking the German Way* (1988). This series also includes books on English, French, Italian, Norwegian, Polish, and Russian cooking.

The Boot

Time Allotment: One or two class periods

Materials: Cardboard, salt dough mixture, maps of Italy, reference materials, paints, food coloring, world maps, globes, pens, pencils, paper

Grade Level: Elementary

Procedure: Have students locate Italy on world maps and globes. Have them pay special attention to the fact that the outline of the country is shaped somewhat like an old-fashioned boot. Next, divide the class into groups and provide them with instructions on making a salt dough map of the country. To tie this map-making activity in with a cultural study, have students paint in a particular section of the country of Italy and investigate the reasons people from that area did or did not emigrate widely to the United States.

Famous Italian Americans: A Timeline

Time Allotment: Two or three class periods

Materials: Reference materials, paper, pens, chart paper, markers, board, chalk

Grade Level: Elementary and middle school

Procedure: Over the years there have been thousands of Italian immigrants to the United States. In addition, there have been a large number of well-known Italian Americans. After an initial discussion, have students identify famous Italian Americans and their contributions or information about them (e.g., birth date, date of contribution, family).
You might use the following chart to help the class get started.

Famous Italian Americans: A Timeline **continued**

Person:	Contribution or Information:
Don Ameche	
Sly Stallone	
John Travolta	
Rocky Marciano	
Constantino Brumidi	
Francis Cabrini	
Frank Sinatra	

AFRICAN AMERICANS

Volumes have been, and continue to be, written about the important role of the African American community in our national culture and as a separate cultural influence. The rich heritage brought to the national culture is vast.

Educators must understand that a large portion of the U.S. citizenry is composed of individuals who have a varied and rich cultural heritage derived from the influences of groups from Africa. As with other ethnic groups, it is important that we understand and help our students in their development of understanding African American heritage.

We tend to focus on the issue of slavery in exploring African American heritage and its effect on culture, but educators must also recognize the various other influences, such as immigration from the West Indies area and how those persons whose ancestry includes free Blacks differ from those of slave heritage (Sowell, 1978). The earliest Africans came to the United States as indentured servants. After a period of time, these individuals received their freedom, and their children were free from birth. It was not until during the late 17th century that the concept of chattel slavery came about. It should be noted, however, that even at this point, slaves could be freed by self-purchase, purchase by free relatives, or reward through special service. Unfortunately, the most common way to become free was by escape.

For slaves who did receive freedom, rights were limited. Voting was usually not permitted, nor was owning land, in some situations, or participating fully in community and other forms of government (i.e., they were not allowed to hold political office or work at government jobs). There were some areas of the United States, however, where free Blacks were able to own land and establish communities. One of these areas was in the Deep South, particularly in the area that is now Louisiana (Sowell, 1978). It should also be pointed out that a number of free Blacks migrated north and became more a part of the mainstream community than their counterparts who remained in parts of the South.

In the first part of the 20th century, there was significant migration of Southern African Americans to the northern part of the United States. This, in itself, proved to be a difficult and often frustrating experience for some (Berry & Blassingame, 1982). Moving from the predominantly rural South to the cities of the North meant adjustments in lifestyle as well as in employment.

Because of this, there were a number of African Americans who took jobs, much like other groups of immigrants before them, that the predominantly white citizenry preferred not to take. Some of these positions included porters on trains, elevator operators, custodians of buildings, and house servants. But within the African American community, there were also a number of carpenters, postal workers, doctors, nurses, barbers, and factory workers.

Although there is a tendency for some people to view the African American community through the images often described by the media (e.g., low income, matriarchal family), it is important to dispel this stereotypical view. Traditionally, education has been an important value for African Americans. In addition, the strong commitment to family and religion should be noted. In the past thirty or so years, a stronger emphasis has been placed on the importance of heritage and culture within the African American community.

By focusing throughout the year-long curriculum on the importance of all cultures and especially the influences of African American culture as a part of social studies activities, educators will help to develop a better long-term understanding in students.

ACTIVITIES

ACTIVITIES RELATED TO AFRICAN AMERICANS
African Freedom Day: May 25

Time Allotment: Two or three class periods

Materials: Reference materials, literature, paper, pencils

Grade Level: Elementary and middle school

Procedure: In celebration of African Freedom Day students can learn about the many differences and likenesses shared by the peoples of Africa. Too often the peoples of Africa have been represented, in books and other media, as barbaric and uncivilized. This is far from reality. By studying this area, students can learn of the influences the traditions have had on African Americans and their U.S. heritage.

Students should develop creative reports about African Freedom Day and other celebrations that have some bearing on the African American citizens of the United States.

Possible Sources:

Marc Bernheim and Evelyn Bernheim. *In Africa.* Atheneum, 1973.
Ashley Bryan. *Lion and the Ostrich Chicks, and other African Tales.* Atheneum, 1986.
John Chaisson. *African Journey.* Bradbury, 1987.

Make a List

Time Allotment: Two or three class periods

Materials: Reference materials, chart paper, markers, pencils, paper

Grade Level: Elementary

Procedure: Make a list of historical and contemporary African Americans who have contributed to African American culture and to the United States in general. Leaders of the past might include George Washington Carver, Frederick Douglass, and so forth. Contemporary African Americans might include Jesse Jackson, Colin Powell, and Oprah Winfrey.

continued

Swahili: A Common Language

Time Allotment: Varied

Materials: Reference materials, charts, chart paper, markers, sentence strips

Grade Level: Elementary

Procedure: Students of all cultures enjoy learning different languages. One of the languages of Africa is Swahili. Although spoken throughout much of East Africa, it serves as a common language among many cultures.

Prepare a chart of common words. Students may replace the American word with its Swahili counterpart.

Swahili Numbers and Words

moja *(mo-jah):* one
mbili *(m-bee-le):* two
tatu *(ta-too):* three
nne *(n-nay):* four
tano *(tah-no):* five
sita *(see-tah):* six
saba *(sah-bah):* seven
nane *(nah-nay):* eight
tisa *(tee-sah):* nine
kumi *(koo-mee):* ten

karibu *(kah-ree-boo):* welcome
jambo *(jam-bow):* hello
mama *(mah-mah):* mother
baba *(bah-bah):* father
kaka *(kah-kah):* brother
dada *(dah-dah):* sister
ngoma *(n-goh-mah):* dance
rafiki *(rah-fee-kee):* friend
kwaheri *(kwa-here-hi):* goodbye
ashante sana (ah-sahn-teh-sah-nah): thanks

From a chart prepared by Social Studies Methods Students—information given to them from a missionary handbook (author unknown).

A Bulletin Board: Famous African Americans

Time Allotment: Four or five class periods

Materials: Bulletin board, reference materials, pencils, paper, markers, construction paper

Grade Level: Elementary and middle school

Procedure: Students should develop a bulletin board about famous African Americans. This could be an ongoing project for a number of days. Divide the class into small groups (or partners). Have the students identify famous African Americans. Then information should be written about each person. (See the attached bulletin board suggestion.)

A Bulletin Board: Famous African Americans **continued**

```
┌──────────────────────────────────────────────────────────────────────┐
│                                                                        │
│   ┌─────────────────┐    ┌──────────────┐    ┌─────────────────┐      │
│   │ Jackie Robinson │    │  Map of      │    │ W.E.B. Du Bois  │      │
│   │ ─────────────── │    │  Africa      │    │ ─────────────── │      │
│   │ ─────────────── │    │              │    │ ─────────────── │      │
│   │ ─────────────── │    └──────────────┘    │ ─────────────── │      │
│   └─────────────────┘                        └─────────────────┘      │
│                                                                        │
│   ┌─────────────────┐                        ┌─────────────────┐      │
│   │ Harriet Tubman  │        African         │ Sojourner Truth │      │
│   │ ─────────────── │       Americans        │ ─────────────── │      │
│   │ ─────────────── │                        │ ─────────────── │      │
│   │ ─────────────── │                        │ ─────────────── │      │
│   └─────────────────┘                        └─────────────────┘      │
│                                                                        │
│                        ┌──────────────┐                               │
│                        │  Timeline    │                               │
│                        │  ──┼──┼──┼──  │                               │
│                        └──────────────┘                               │
│                                                                        │
│   ┌─────────────────┐                 ┌────────────────────┐          │
│   │ Louis Armstrong │                 │ Martin Luther King,│          │
│   │ ─────────────── │                 │ Jr.                │          │
│   │ ─────────────── │                 │ ──────────────────  │          │
│   │ ─────────────── │                 │ ──────────────────  │          │
│   └─────────────────┘                 └────────────────────┘          │
│                                                                        │
└──────────────────────────────────────────────────────────────────────┘
```

JEWISH AMERICANS

For some, when the term "Jewish" is mentioned, visions of men wearing little round caps, people lighting candles, and religious leaders singing nonfamiliar songs or chants come to mind. Unfortunately, for some, ideas of selfish people or people who want the best price for a product come to mind. For educators, it is important to dispel these stereotypical views and move our students to better understanding.

Jewish Americans are different from other major cultural groups in that their heritage is linked to religion rather than a particular nation or country. Because the predominant makeup of the citizenry of the United States is Christian–Anglo-Saxon, and the identity of Jewish Americans is basically a religious foundation, misunderstanding has often developed. If we are to help our students learn about the culture, it is important that we have some basic knowledge ourselves.

First, in exploring the Jewish American heritage, there are various areas that may be of importance. One such area is immigration. There have been at least three major groups of Jewish immigrants coming to the United States. The first group was the Sephardic Jews, primarily from Spain and Portugal; the German Jews, the second group; and the third group, Eastern European Jews, primarily from Russia. The Central and Eastern European Jews were of Ashkenazic Jewish heritage (Bennett, 1990).

Like a number of other immigrant groups, the first Jewish Americans came to this country primarily for religious reasons. They brought with them an emphasis on economic success as well as the need to be able to practice their religious beliefs without the fear of being persecuted. Prior to the Revolutionary War, these first immigrants had regained much of the financial losses experienced by coming to a new country (Sowell, 1980). They tended to develop close community relations, focusing on their culture and family.

The second group of Jewish Americans, those primarily of German Jewish heritage, did not settle quite as much in close communities with others of the same heritage. Instead, they tended to live within already established communities, regardless of the heritage of their neighbors. These immigrants, while still maintaining their faith and culture, were active in the general society and appeared to be somewhat assimilated in this respect (Sowell, 1981).

Because of their role not only in the Jewish American community but as businessmen and successful professionals, they were somewhat embarrassed by the third group of Jewish American immigrants (Sowell, 1981). The Eastern European Jewish immigrants fled to this country to escape from persecution. Because of their peasant background, as well as their strong commitment to their faith, they lived in crowded communities, many near the garment industries of New York and other northeastern cities. Much like a number of immigrant groups before them, they took jobs that other citizens did not want.

Although it is clear that there has always been diversity within the Jewish American community, it is important to point out that unity also exists. As a cultural group, Jewish Americans are well known for their humanitarianism and commitment to human rights issues. In addition, there is a unity that Jewish Americans share as the result of having a common belief system that is unlike the major population of the United States.

In considering the role of Jewish Americans within our national culture, it is important for our students to develop a better understanding of their culture and to view each person as an individual.

ACTIVITIES

ACTIVITIES RELATED TO JEWISH AMERICANS
Make A Dreidel

Time Allotment: Flexible

Materials: Copies of the dreidel pattern (see attached), scissors, glue, markers, crayons, appropriate children's literature selections

Grade Level: Elementary

Procedure: Before beginning this activity, explain to the class the significance of dreidels to people of Jewish faith. Be sure students understand the legend; this may best be accomplished through the use of children's literature selections. (Check with your school librarian or the public library to see what is available.)

Next have the students make their own dreidels. To construct the dreidel, they should follow these directions:

1. Cut out the dreidel pattern carefully, especially the little stars on the top and bottom flaps.
2. Fold back on all the dotted lines, and paste the dreidel together.
3. Make a blunt point on a stick, and put it through the stars. If the stick doesn't stay in place, you may use tape. (If a stick is not available or does not work, you can use a toothpick or a short pencil.)

Variation: A game to play with the dreidel.

Each player gets five pieces of candy. Next each player places two pieces of candy in the "pot." Everyone spins their dreidel starting with the tallest (or youngest, oldest, wearing a certain color, or hair length) player. If you spin:

Gimel—you win all the candy
He—you win half the candy
Nun—you win nothing
Shin—you place two more pieces of candy in the pot

Make A Dreidel **continued**

The game continues until all the pieces of candy have been used. Items other than candy may be used.

Dreidel Pattern

Hanukkah Cookies

Time Allotment: One class period

Materials: Ingredients for Hanukkah cookies (see recipe), oven, additional adult help, paper plates, napkins, water (for cleaning up)

Grade Level: Elementary

Procedure: Some families eat special foods on special days. Students may discuss the special foods they have. Following this discussion, be sure that students have an understanding of the significance of Hanukkah for the Jewish people before completing this activity.

Hanukkah Cookies **continued**

Hanukkah Cookies

Ingredients:	Equipment:
2 cups flour	large bowl
1 cup sugar	measuring cup
1/2 teaspoon salt	measuring spoons
2 teaspoons baking powder	beater
1 egg	sifter
1/3 cup butter	bread board
1/4 cup milk	rolling pin
1 teaspoon vanilla	cookie cutters
butter, oil or shortening	cookie sheet

Directions:

1. Preheat oven to 350° F.
2. Cream butter and sugar in a large bowl.
3. In another bowl, beat the egg and add the milk and vanilla.
4. Stir both mixtures into a large bowl.
5. Sift together the flour, salt, and baking powder.
6. Add these ingredients into the large mixture and stir well.
7. Place the dough in the refrigerator for one hour.
8. Dust a bread board and rolling pin with flour.
9. Roll out the cool dough about 1/4 of an inch thick.
10. Cut with cookie cutters.
11. Place on greased cookie sheet.
12. Bake in oven for 12 minutes.

NOTE: If cookie cutters are not available, appropriate designs may be cut from heavy cardboard and students may trace around them in the dough with a dull or plastic knife.

Rosh Hashanah: Jewish New Year

Time Allotment: One or two class periods

Materials: Copies of shofar puzzle, scissors, construction paper, markers, crayons, glue

Grade Level: Elementary

Procedure: Discuss with students how they celebrate the New Year. For some, the traditional activities of fireworks and football will surely be mentioned.

The Jewish New Year is a quiet time of serious meditation. It is a holy day, considered the birthday of the world as well as the beginning of a new year on the Hebrew calendar.

Rosh Hashanah: Jewish New Year **continued**

"Rosh" means "head" and "shanah" means "year." It offers the opportunity of taking spiritual stock of oneself. A comparison might be made to how New Year's resolutions are plans for changes in one's life.

Be prepared to give students some background information concerning Rosh Hashanah. Explain that the shofar is a significant part of this occasion. If possible, read a story or watch a film concerning the importance of the shofar.

Shofar Puzzle Pattern

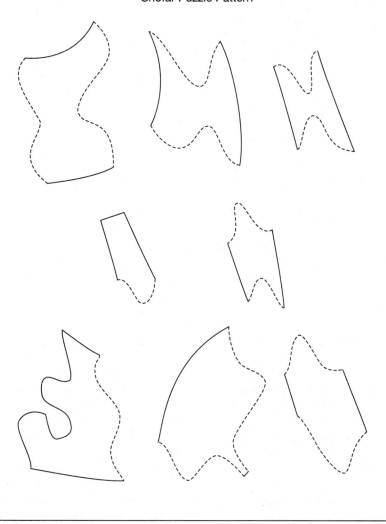

Rosh Hashanah: Jewish New Year **continued**

As a follow-up activity, the students may make a shofar puzzle.

1. Cut out the jigsaw pieces carefully.
2. Fit them together in the shape of a shofar.
3. Glue the pieces on construction paper.
4. Color the shofar. (These may also be laminated.)

Forgiveness and Understanding

Time Allotment: Flexible

Materials: Books appropriate for older students, questions to prompt discussion, paper, pencils and pens

Grade Level: Middle school

Procedure: Israel was established in 1948 when few countries would admit the large numbers of Jewish refugees. From what were they trying to get away? Read appropriate stories as a class. Follow each session with an opportunity to discuss and reflect in a journal-type writing assignment.

Appropriate selections might include:

Linda Atkinson. *In Kindling Flame.* Lothrop, 1984.
Anne Frank. *The Diary of a Young Girl.* Doubleday, 1952.

NOTE: This can be a sensitive subject. Use your knowledge of your students and your professional judgement.

*A number of educational videos are also available through various professional organizations. These may be used rather than reading selections.

NATIVE AMERICANS

In recent years, the media, especially the television and movie industry, has been more factual in representation of Native Americans. The portrayal of "Indians" as being savages and aggressors in the history of the United States has been minimized. In considering the rich heritage of the Native American culture, it is important that we, as educators, have a basic knowledge.

First, we need to understand that the term Native American does not have the same meaning to all. In some instances those persons who *identify* themselves as native are such, but in other cases only those of full native heritage are recognized (Hirschfelder, 1982). Because of this diversity in opinion, it is important to help students understand how various views may be acceptable, determined only by the situation.

Second, we need to look at our understanding of Native Americans and what really happened, from a historical perspective. It is important that we look at the information in our social studies texts as well as other reference materials to see what is mentioned in terms of treaties or other government actions taken in relation to Native Americans. We need to be able to discuss the information not only from the Anglo perspective but from the Native American perspective. For example, the Northwest Ordinance as it was written basically respected the rights of Native Americans; but was it enforced as written, or did the images of savages attacking early settlers lead to later actions, such as the Indian Removal Act (McNickle, 1972; Vogel, 1972)? It is important to help our students learn accurately about the role the U.S. government did, and did not, play in determining many of the stereotypical views held by people even today.

In looking at the Native American population of today, we need to think in terms of the lifestyle of those persons who live on reservations in comparison to those who live in other places. There have been changes in the past twenty or so years to help Native Americans who live in either place become more aware of the importance of their heritage. There are now more tribal celebrations, more education concerning the belief systems of the Native American heritage, as well as language instruction so that native languages are not lost ("Wind River," 1985; Forbes, 1973).

We must help students develop a more accurate understanding of the role Native Americans had in the initial and continued success of the United States. Taking this into consideration helps to dispel the stereotypical views often held in the past. It is important to help students, even at the elementary and middle school levels, recognize the contributions of Native Americans in various terms including (but not limited to) exploration, patterns of settlement, and foods (Billman, 1992).

ACTIVITIES

ACTIVITIES RELATED TO NATIVE AMERICANS
Names of Places

Time Allotment: Two or three class periods
Materials: Reference materials, U.S. map, markers, pens, paper
Grade Level: Elementary and middle school

Procedure: Many names of states, rivers, and cities come from Native American languages. After introducing students to this information, they should investigate to increase their knowledge. Places should be labeled on a U.S. map (e.g., Massachusetts; Ohio River; Pontiac, Michigan).

A Mural

Time Allotment: Three or four class periods

Materials: Large butcher paper, markers, crayons, pencils, writing paper

Grade Level: Elementary

Procedure: After the students have completed an initial study of Native American lifestyles, have them plan murals. Each group should develop a mural on each of the seven major Native American cultural areas of the United States. Students should make their murals as accurate as possible by using information from reference materials. In addition, a short report may be developed to explain the mural.

Storytelling—Native American Style

Time Allotment: Varied

Materials: Stories appropriate for storytelling. Possible suggestions:

Trickster Tales from Prairie Lodgefires. Bernice Anderson, Abdington, 1979.

The Whistling Skeleton. George Grinell, Four Winds, 1982.

Raven the Trickster: Legends of the North American Indians. Gail Robinson, Atheneum, 1982.

Grade Level: Elementary and middle school

Procedure: Explain to the students that Native American storytellers developed styles of telling stories over a long period of time. Stories were carefully handed down from one generation to the next. There were a variety of ways in which stories were begun or ended. Also, some Native American storytellers used gestures to increase the dramatic effect, while others varied their rhythm.

After this introduction, tell the class a number of Native American stories or have a guest to do so (a cultural representative or an actor).

Why Masks?

Time Allotment: Three or four class periods

Materials: Heavy cardboard, elastic, string, paint, markers, reference materials

Grade Level: Elementary

Why Masks? **continued**

> **Procedure:**   Face painting and wearing of masks are important in many Native American cultural celebrations and ceremonies. After an initial study, students should use reference materials to learn more about masks and their importance.
>
> As a follow up or culmination of their research, they should make masks. These will not be authentic because they will be made of heavy cardboard, but it is important that the students follow the information in the reference materials concerning the shape and drawings on the masks.
>
> ## *Timeline*
>
> **Time Allotment:**   Four or five class periods
>
> **Materials:**   Reference materials, large butcher paper, markers
>
> **Grade Level:**   Upper elementary and middle school
>
> **Procedure:**   Too many times the heritage of Native Americans is viewed from the perspective made possible through movies. Our students deserve more than this often stereotypical information.
>
> Divide the class into several groups, one for each Native American cultural group, if possible. Each group should be responsible for developing a timeline of important events for that group being investigated.

ASIAN AMERICANS

The term Asian American is one which often brings to mind, for elementary and middle school students, thoughts of the latest karate action film they have seen. Some of us think of the people we last encountered at an oriental restaurant. In either case, these are representations that form the foundation for the view and understanding of Asian Americans.

In developing a more accurate view of Asian Americans, it is first important to recognize that there are several different groups that make up the Asian American community. These groups include persons of Chinese, Japanese, Korean, Filipino, and Indochinese (i.e., from areas such as Vietnam, Laos, and Cambodia) heritage ("Asians: To America," 1985). The three most prominent groups nationwide are the Chinese, Japanese, and Indochinese American groups.

The first Asian immigrants were mostly from China. These were often young men sent by their families to work for monetary gain after the opening of China in the 1800s. It was not the plan for them to become permanent residents, but only to work for a while and then return to their families. The two areas of work in which they found themselves were in the railroad industry and work related to gold mining in California.

Over a period of time these men became more permanent residents; however, they were not allowed to become citizens nor were they allowed to bring their families to the United States. This anti-Asian feeling spread to the first Japanese that came to the United States.

Much like the first Chinese immigrants, the first Japanese came to the United States to gain wealth and then return to their native country. Again, more permanent residence became a reality for many of these young Japanese men; however, the earlier laws that forbade the Chinese from bringing their families to the United States were retracted or reworded concerning the Japanese immigrants so that families could be brought to the United States. Later naturalization was allowed, and the number of Japanese American citizens increased.

Members of the Japanese American community are often viewed as a model minority because of several characteristics they demonstrate, such as being hard-working and accepting of the team approach for success, which is often required in order to succeed in our national culture. According to information compiled by Feagin, Japanese Americans have the highest literacy rate of the major cultural groups in our society (Feagin, 1978). In addition a large percentage of Japanese Americans appear to have adopted the language, religion, and general societal views of the national culture.

The third and most recent group of Asian immigrants to come to the United States are those of Indochinese heritage. Prior to the fall of Saigon, at the end of the Vietnam War, the numbers were only in the tens of thousands; however this number grew into the hundreds of thousands within the short period of 1975 to 1976, causing a great deal of frustration not only for the new immigrants, but for the United States government and the communities in which resettlement communities were established (Thuy, 1983). The original plan to resettle these new immigrants throughout the United States was not a long-term reality as with many of the other major cultural groups. The desire to live near others of shared background for economical and social reasons, which had been expressed by other immigrant groups, also motivated the Indochinese refugees and immigrants. Therefore, they have moved into various cities and locations to be near others of the same culture.

Prejudice and discrimination were and still are, problems for a number of these new immigrants, but overall, not to the same extent as for the Chinese and Japanese. One of the greatest concerns was to learn English as quickly as possible. This of course has been an area of concern for public schools in the United States. It is also important to note that the misunderstanding of cultural differences has caused many of the newer citizens to isolate themselves. It is important that we, as educators, help our students learn that differences should be respected, not degraded. By having the students actively involved in learning experiences, such learning can take place more easily.

ACTIVITIES

ACTIVITIES RELATED TO ASIAN AMERICANS
The First Chinese Immigrants

Time Allotment: Two or three class periods

Materials: Reference materials, pens, paper, chart paper, markers

Grade Level: Upper elementary and middle school

Procedure: Have students read about Chinese immigration to this country in order to learn how rapidly this occurred. (Note especially the effects of the discovery of gold in California and the building of the transcontinental railroad.) Develop charts about the immigration facts. Develop charts concerning the special characteristics of the early Chinese immigrants (e.g., single young men, lived in dormitory-like housing).

Traditional Chinese Celebrations

Time Allotment: Flexible

Materials: Reference materials

Grade Level: Elementary and middle school

Procedure: Many Chinese Americans still celebrate the traditional holidays and festivals of China. These often involve special symbols, and special foods are eaten. Help students identify some of the major holidays. They should use reference materials to learn more about the holidays.

Suggestions to help get the class started: Chinese New Year, Spring Festival, The Dragon Boat Festival, Festival of the Moon, Winter Festival. This is a great activity in which to involve a resource speaker!

"Me": An Individual Within a Dual Culture

Time Allotment: Two or three class periods

Materials: Chart paper, markers, pictures, glue, reference materials

Grade Level: Elementary and middle school

Procedure: Generalizing across Asian American customs and cultures can have a negative effect on the self-esteem of the individual and may undermine the development of cultural understanding in the group. In implementing an activity where all students are involved in developing a collage of photographs and other information, the Asian American (in this particular activity, Korean American) student will have a nonthreatening way to be recognized as an individual.

Children's Festival

Time Allotment: Two or three class periods

Materials: Reference materials, art supplies

Grade Level: Elementary

Procedure: May 5 is the celebration of the Children's Festival in Japan. This is one of many celebrations that Japanese Americans often celebrate. Have students research information about the festival and prepare a celebration. (See patterns for carp kites and streamers.)

Traditional Values: Vietnam

Time Allotment: Two or three class periods

Materials: Reference materials, chart paper, markers

Grade Level: Upper elementary and middle school

Procedure: Select folktales from Vietnam. Read to the class or have students read the folktales and identify the values in the literature. Students should make a chart of their ideas. Possible questions to help students identify values could include:

1. What is the desired reward?
2. What actions are rewarded?
3. What actions are punished?
4. What rewards are given to the hero or heroine?
5. What are the personal characteristics of people in the story?

CUBAN AMERICANS

For those of us who were around in the late 1950s and early 1960s, the mention of Cuba reminds us of the threat of Soviet warfare during the Cuban Crisis, and for some of us, Desi Arnaz, Ricky of "I Love Lucy" fame. For those of us who were aware in the early 1980s, we are more familiar with the boatlift in which thousands of Cubans came into the United States. In either situation, the view of Cuban immigration was somewhat limited and stereotypical.

There have been two major waves of immigration from Cuba. The first Cubans came to the United States during the period after the takeover of Cuba by Fidel Castro and the communist regime. The general makeup of these immigrants was middle class. They were more concerned about freedom than economy (Diaz, 1987). A large percentage of this group did not have to wait for visas, and the restrictions experienced by a number of other immigrant groups, such as the Asian Americans, were not employed.

The second large group of Cubans to arrive in the United States came in the early 1980s. This group consisted largely of people who were less educated and not as affluent as the first Cubans to arrive. Although there was much discussion of the criminals included in this wave of immigrants, in reality, the term was used to describe all persons that had previously been held in Cuban detention centers, many of whom would not be considered criminals in the United States (Diaz, 1987).

According to Olson, Cuban Americans are the third largest Spanish speaking group in the United States. Like a number of other cultural groups, Cuban Americans often live near one another. One reason for this is their strong commitment to their cultural heritage. In addition, Cuban Americans are "unashamedly patriotic, grateful to the United States for their freedom." (Olson, 1979).

This, along with the fact that Cuban Americans, in general, also wish to maintain their native language (Spanish), has important ramifications for educators. It is very important that students learn about the culture of Cuban Americans and avoid development of stereotypical viewpoints.

ACTIVITIES

ACTIVITIES RELATED TO CUBAN AMERICANS

Language

Time Allotment: One or two class periods

Materials: Charts, markers, reference materials

Grade Level: Elementary

Procedure: There are many dialects of Spanish spoken among the various cultural groups who live in the United States. Identify terms and have students investigate the linguistic differences between Cuban Americans and other Latin American citizens.

Immigration from Cuba

Time Allotment: Two or three class periods

Immigration from Cuba **continued**

Materials: Butcher paper, markers, paper, pens, pencils

Grade Level: Upper elementary and middle school

Procedure: Divide the class into small groups. After an initial discussion about the takeover of Cuba, present the following senario:

Your family is forced to move to a country in which the language and customs are different. You are allowed to take only a few clothes. All other possessions are left behind forever because you cannot return. Describe what your life might be like where you are going. What clothing would you take with you? Why? How well do you think your family would get along? What kinds of adjustments would you have to make?

Students should answer the questions through illustrations, written responses, and discussion.

The Holidays of Cuba

Time Allotment: Four or five class periods

Materials: Reference materials

Grade Level: Elementary

Procedure: Depending on the level of assimilation, many Cuban American families celebrate holidays particular to the culture of Cuba. Help students identify holidays and how they are traditionally celebrated within the Cuban American culture.

After research is completed, each group should present information culminating with a day of celebration where each group will celebrate a holiday, as well as invite the whole class. This should be an ongoing study and accuracy should be of significance. This is a great time for resource persons to visit and share their knowledge.

What Happened in 1959 (in Cuba)?

Time Allotment: Varied

Materials: Reference materials, interviews, pens, pencils, paper

Grade Level: Middle school

Procedure: Many students in today's middle school classrooms have no clear understanding of the problems encountered by the Cuban people as a result of the Castro revolution. Following an initial introduction to the information, students should discuss and write about their feelings or viewpoints. Resource speakers may be invited to supply firsthand accounts of the events of 1959.

MEXICAN AMERICANS

Ask your students to describe a Mexican American and, unfortunately, the stereotypical characterization of sombrero-wearing people will, in many instances, be a part of the description given. Depending on the makeup of your class and school, the description could be of a peer that the students view as a friend and companion. In either situation, it is important that we, as educators, make every effort to dispel the myths of stereotypical ideas.

In preparing to teach about Mexican Americans we might first look at the historical background of this important cultural group. According to McWilliams, Mexican American history actually dates back to 1500 B.C. and the Mayan civilization. From there, Mexican American history continues through to the Aztec empire and the rule of Montezuma II. When Cortez conquered Mexico in 1521, the beginning of three hundred years of Spanish rule came about (McWilliams, 1968).

Later when the United States annexed the territory that is now Texas, the treaty of Guadalupe Hidalgo, which guaranteed full citizenship including rights for landowners, was supposed to protect the Mexican Americans who lived on the land annexed. This was not a reality. This treatment of the cultural group differs from treatment of several other immigrant groups in that they were annexed with the territory.

While there is no acceptable excuse, Mexican American immigrants experienced a great amount of prejudice and discrimination throughout the 1900s. Even as we move into the next century, there are marked differences in the lifestyle and economic standing of a large portion of the Mexican American community in comparison to that of other cultural groups (Acuna, 1988).

Cultural heritage is strongly emphasized by the Mexican American community. Customs, language, and religion are areas that a number of Mexican Americans wish their children would maintain. Biculturalism is preferred in many Mexican American homes (Feagin, 1978).

Because of these facts, along with the general need for preparing our elementary and middle school students for citizenship in a global society, we must recognize the cultural importance of Mexican Americans as productive contributors and members of our society.

ACTIVITIES

ACTIVITIES RELATED TO MEXICAN AMERICANS
Cinco de Mayo (May 5)

Time Allotment: Four or five class periods

Materials: Large butcher paper, markers, crayons, reference materials

Grade Level: Elementary

Cinco de Mayo (May 5) **continued**

Procedure: First students should learn why May 5 is so important in Mexico and Mexican American culture. (The victory of Mexican forces over the French at Puebla, Mexico occurred on May 5, 1862.) Students should make murals representing the events that led up to the victory as well as how the holiday is celebrated today. Group work is recommended.

Constitution Day—Mexico

Time Allotment: Flexible

Materials: Reference materials, writing materials, various props

Grade Level: Middle school

Procedure: First students should learn why February 5 is important in Mexico and to Mexican Americans. Students should develop reports concerning the events that led to the celebration. Short skits concerning the events should be developed by students.

The Importance of Art

Time Allotment: Varied

Materials: Various art supplies, reference materials

Grade Level: Lower elementary

Procedure: Art is important in any culture. One form of art that has gained interest is mosaics. Students should look at works of various artists. One artist of particular importance in Mexico and Mexican American heritage is Diego Rivera, who designed the Olympic Stadium in Mexico City.

After students have completed their research, they should be able to make their own mosaics using construction paper, colored crushed egg shells, wrapping paper, or foil. This will further their understanding of the art form.

NAFTA: What, When, Where, Who, Why?

Time Allotment: Two or three class periods

Materials: Reference materials, chart paper, markers, chalk, chalkboard

Grade Level: Middle school

Procedure: The United States has many trade agreements with countries all over the globe. One that is especially important to Mexicans, Americans, and Mexican Americans is the North American Free Trade Agreement (NAFTA). Students should first brainstorm about what they know or think they know about NAFTA and its effects.

After a brainstorming session, questions should be developed under the heading: what, when, where, who, and why. Divide the class into groups and have each group investigate.

NAFTA: What, When, Where, Who, Why? **continued**

After the research is completed, students should compare the ideas they had before and after their investigation.

Famous Mexican Americans

Time Allotment: Two or three class periods

Materials: Reference materials, art supplies, pens, pencils, paper

Grade Level: Elementary and middle school

Procedure: After a study of the various contributions Mexican Americans have brought to our country, each group of students should decide on one person they would like to investigate and share with the class. Rather than just have the usual written or oral reports, students should develop a scrapbook of information about the person. This should include illustrations (drawn or cut from magazines) as well as written captions.

The scrapbook should have a cassette tape on which each caption is read and additional information is given. (Also, students should indicate on the audio tape when to turn the page.)

NOTE: This would be a great study-buddy project matching younger and older students.

HISPANIC AMERICANS

One of the problems facing educators in talking with students about the Hispanic culture is a clear definition of Hispanics. According to a report by Kosmin and Lachman, the United States Census Bureau results for 1990 did not include a clear definition of Hispanics, but maintained that they could be of any race (Kosman & Lachman, 1993). As with a number of other major cultural groups within the makeup of the United States national culture, Hispanic people may be members of various groups that have immigrated to the United States over a long period of time, or they may be recent immigrants. The countries of origin may include, but not be limited to, Puerto Rico, Haiti, El Salvador, Colombia, or other countries in and around Central and South America ("Hispanics: A Melding," 1985).

In learning about the Hispanic culture, there are some similarities that may be focused upon. One of these is a general belief system that emphasizes individualism, self-respect, and a general respect for nature. In addition, many of the cultures represented within the Hispanic culture share religion (i.e., Catholicism) and core family value systems that are supported by the religious beliefs (Olson, 1979).

Assimilation of Hispanic Americans into the national culture has varied depending on the individuals and the area in which they have settled. Like a number of other immigrant groups, a number of Hispanics have taken jobs that others prefer not to take. In addition, for new immigrants the language barrier has been an area of concern. Because of the language barrier as well as the safety of living near those with similar beliefs and values, a number of Hispanics have elected to live in communities made up of those of similar heritage. This is not to imply that all Hispanic Americans live in these places; however, it is important for educators to be aware of this as well as help their students to be aware.

It is important for educators working with Hispanic American students, as with all students, to learn as much as possible about their individual needs and cultural beliefs. This is of great importance especially with the later immigrants because of the dropout rate. According to Kunisawa, the number of Hispanic students who do not complete high school outranks all other groups. This is, in part, a problem of cultural misunderstanding (Kunisawa, 1988). Educators must help students of all cultural backgrounds to understand that they may be a part of more than one culture, that is the culture of their heritage and the national culture (Melendez, Melendez, & Molina, 1981). It is equally important that we, as educators, help students respect the different needs of all students.

ACTIVITIES

ACTIVITIES RELATED TO HISPANIC AMERICANS
Emancipation Day

Time Allotment: One or two class periods

Materials: Reference materials, videos or films, chart paper, markers, pencils, paper

Grade Level: Elementary

Procedure: Have students explore the importance of Emancipation Day (March 22) for Puerto Rico and for Puerto Ricans living in the United States. Be sure to help students develop an understanding of the events that led up to this day. If possible show a film or video about how Emancipation Day is celebrated in Puerto Rico and the United States. Students may draw illustrations to show how the day is celebrated based on the information in reference materials.

continued

Place of Origin

Time Allotment: Two or three class periods

Materials: Reference materials, drawing paper, markers, pens, pencils, writing paper

Grade Level: Upper elementary and middle school

Procedure: Hispanic American students often have questions about their country or origin. This activity may be an individual or group activity in which students investigate specific questions. General questions to investigate might include: What is the place like? What are the people like? and What is the history of the place? Students may answer the questions and follow up with written poems, stories, or drawings to represent their findings.

   (This activity is especially helpful for students who are unfamiliar with their country of origin.)

My Family

Time Allotment: Two or three class periods

Materials: Writing materials, reference materials

Grade Level: Elementary

Procedure: One common element shared by many Hispanic Americans is a strong commitment to family. In helping students explore information about their families, many accomplishments that have been achieved may be discovered. Special emphasis should be given to individual accomplishments (e.g., graduated from college, first work experience). Other areas that might be included in the study should be how names are chosen, where the family lived in their native country, and so on.

Spanish in the Classroom

Time Allotment: Two or three class periods

Materials: Appropriate reference materials, charts, writing paper, pencils

Grade Level: Elementary

Procedure: Whether or not there are Spanish-speaking students in the classroom, it is important to expose students to Spanish. Have the students learn simple phrases and develop charts. Information might be obtained from books, recordings, or other resources.

Haitian Immigrants

Time Allotment: One or two class periods

Materials: Reference materials, writing paper, chart paper, markers, pencils, pens

Haitian Immigrants **continued**

> **Grade Level:**   Upper elementary and middle school
>
>   **Procedure:**   In the past decade there has been an increase in the number of immigrants from the island country of Haiti. Students need to learn about these later immigrants. Areas to be explored include why the people left Haiti, how the majority left, difficulties they encountered in leaving and in coming to the United States, and what has happened to them since arriving. Students may demonstrate their findings by developing charts, illustrations, written reports, poems, or stories.

HELPFUL HINTS FOR UNIT 6:

1. In looking back at your school experiences, what do you remember about multicultural education as a part of social studies? What do you want your students to remember?
2. Develop a list of cultural groups you need to become more familiar with in order to provide your students with more accurate information. Design and implement a timeline and plan for increasing your knowledge.
3. Given the cultural makeup of your area, are there any additional groups you feel merit study? If so, plan four activities that might be used to help students develop a better understanding of the group.
4. Visit a local cultural center. How could this cultural center be presented so that elementary or middle school students would benefit from a visit?

REFERENCES

Acuna, R. (1988). *Occupied America: A history of Chicanas* (3rd ed.). New York: Harper & Row.

Asians: To America with skills. (1985, July). *Time*, pp. 44–46.

Baruth, L. & Manning, M. L. (1992). *Multicultural education of children and adolescents*. (p. 23). Needham Heights, MA: Allyn & Bacon.

Bennett, C. (1990). *Comprehensive multicultural education: Theory and practice* (2nd ed.). Boston: Allyn & Bacon.

Berry, M. F. & Blassingame, J. W. (1982). *Long memory: The Black experience in America*. New York: Oxford Press.

Billman, J. (1992). The Native American curriculum: Attempting alternatives to tepees and headbands. *Young Children, 47* (6), 22–25.

Diaz, C. (1987). Puerto Ricans in the United States: Concepts, strategies, and materials. In J.A. Banks (Ed.), *Teaching strategies for ethnic studies.* Newton, MA: Allyn & Bacon.

Feagin, J. (1978). *Racial and ethnic relations.* Englewood Cliffs, NJ: Prentice Hall.

Forbes, J. D. (1972). Teaching Native American values and cultures. In J. A. Banks (Ed.), *Teaching ethnic studies: Concepts and strategies.* Washington, D.C.: National Council for the Social Studies.

Hernandez, H. (1989). *Multicultural education: A teacher's guide to content and process.* Columbus, OH: Merrill.

Hirschfelder, A. (1982). *Happily may I walk: American Indians and Alaska natives today.* New York: Charles Scribner.

Hispanics: A melding of cultures. (1985, July). *Time,* p. 36.

Kosmin, B. A. & Lachman, S. P. (1993). *One nation under God: Religion in contemporary American society.* New York: Harmony Books.

Kunisawa, B. (1988). A nation in crisis: the dropout dilemma. *NEA Today, 1.*

Lay-Dopyera & Dopyera, J. (1987). *Becoming a teacher of young children* (3rd ed.). New York: Random House.

Melendez, D., Melendez, D. C., & Molina, A. (1981). Pluralism and the Hispanic student: Challenge to educators. *Theory Into Practice, 20* (1), 89.

McNickle, D. (1971). Indian and European: Indian–White relations from discovery to 1887. In D. E. Walker, Jr. (Ed.), *The emergent Native Americans* (pp. 75–86). Boston: Little Brown.

McWilliams, C. (1968). *North from Mexico: the Spanish-speaking people of the United States.* New York: Greenwood Press.

Olson, J. S. (1979). *Ethnic America: A history.* New York: Basic Books.

Parnell, H. (1988) *Cooking the German way.* Minneapolis: Lerner.

Sowell, T. (ed.). (1978). *Essays and data on American ethnic groups.* Washington, D.C.: The Urban Institute.

Sowell, T. (1981). Ethnic America: A history. New York: Basic Books.

Thuy, V. G. (1983). The Indochinese in America: Who are they and how are they doing. In D. T. Nakanishi and M. Hirano-Nakanishi (Eds.), *The education of Asian and Pacific Americans: Historical perspective and prescriptions for the future.* Phoenix, AZ: Oryx Press.

Vogel, V. J. (1972). *This country was ours.* New York: Harper & Row.

Wind River's last generation. (1985, October). *Time,* p. 40.

Zangwill, I. (1909). *The Melting Pot* (play).

Pulling It All Together

SUMMARY OF INFORMATION

In Unit One, we developed a working definition of social studies to include a study of the past and present and the study of social and life skills needed by global citizens. As we look back over the information covered in this project, we need to explore how educators might pull all this together and really begin to take steps towards accomplishing this task.

First and foremost in working with students in the area of social studies, or any curriculum area, is to look at our own styles of teaching, the information we are hoping to help our students explore, and our own knowledge of the information. It is sad to enter a classroom where the teacher really knows better, but is teaching based only on the information provided by the text, which the students could very well explore for themselves. In rethinking all the information covered, the goal is to take the information in this project and branch out depending on the knowledge you already have as well as the information your students need to know.

Second, we need to rethink our perception of the students we work with. Are those teaching styles we employ actually working? Will those teaching strategies we now use involve the students so that they will be active learners? Do we understand the cultural influences that may be affecting our students? Do we treat all students the same? While not all of this information is provided in this project, there is a starting point for future and current classroom professionals. For example, there are a number of activities in several sections that are designed to help "get the ball rolling" by providing for active involvement on the part of students. In addition, there are sections that provide thumbnail sketches of various cultural influences or heritages that affect our students and ourselves.

One section that sets this project apart from some others is Unit Five, which deals with religion. We, as educators, must understand that as we move into the next century and as we prepare students for their role as global citizens, we must not be afraid to address issues that for a number of years have been ignored for fear of making someone uncomfortable. Understanding can only become a reality when we learn about one another. Religion is a part of the daily lives of a large group of the students we work with at the elementary and middle school levels. The cultural attributes of religion must be understood. In thinking about including some level of instruction about religion, it is important to reemphasize that as teachers our role is to distance ourselves from our beliefs and focus only on the cultural aspects. We want to prepare our students and help them overcome stereotypical viewpoints, not convert them to some belief system.

Every day through the national or world news we hear, see, or read about various incidents involving our fellow human beings. When we stop to consider that a large percentage of these incidents involve some degree of cultural influence or a cultural group that is represented somewhere in the national culture of the United States, it is important that we try to develop a basic knowledge so that we can help our students be better informed citizens of today and tomorrow.

In Unit Six, a number of the cultural groups that make up the historical and contemporary society of the United States are discussed. This section, much like Unit Five, is designed to give educators a brief background of the various cultural groups as well as a look at a number of activities to begin the study to help students become more aware of the positive influences heritage has on their role as citizens. In thinking about Unit Six, educators need to consider the makeup of their class and the community in which they work. Although no one group or influence is more important than another, more emphasis may need to be devoted to a particular study of heritage and cultural background in order to promote more understanding.

When looking at the various cultures represented in the heritage of the citizenry of the United States, it is vital that students have some level of understanding related to the world. In order to attain understanding, students need to be familiar with skills related to the study of maps and globes. Unit Three is devoted to helping students learn about the many skills involved in using maps and globes. Rather than go over all the information provided, a summary of the information is simple. In order for students to learn through the use of these valuable tools, the educator must start out with basic skills and move students toward independent use of the materials to help them in learning information. We must look at the maturity and ability levels of the students and decide on information they need to learn in order to move forward. It is also important that we remember all students are not at the same place in their development, so review and remediation is a natural and normal part of map and globe instruction.

An area of the curriculum which is a natural for helping students learn information in the area of social studies is that of language arts. While we have a tendency to focus more on using the various areas of language arts in reading instruction, it is important to note that each of the areas—listening, speaking, and writing—may also be effectively used as a part of social studies instruction. Unit Four is designed to help educators rethink how they have used or plan to use language arts as a part of social studies instruction.

In addition to providing a number of suggestions concerning the various language arts areas, Unit Four also provides a rationale for using literature as a part of social studies instruction. It is important for educators to help students develop accurate perceptions of the world around them. One source that may be beneficial in accomplishing this task is children's literature. Trade books, or library books as they are often called by students, are helpful as additional resource tools as well as for providing narrative presentation of information that may be somewhat confusing or disjointed for some students when encountered in the social studies text or some reference materials.

In considering the role of the social studies text as a part of instruction, Unit Two deals with the various components and how they may be effectively used. While some experienced and even novice educators may feel that they know all about published programs, it is, on occasion, good for us to rethink our views of the components. Although this section may seem to be unimportant to those of us who have used published programs in the past, it is important for novice educators to think carefully about how they might use the materials in their initial teaching experiences.

One point that seems important to reemphasize is that social studies textbook publishers most often do not plan for their published programs to be the only tool used in the classroom setting for social studies instruction. Great strides have been made in improving the content and design of published programs, but again, the importance of providing for the individual needs of the students should be a factor in helping decide how to most effectively use the materials provided by textbook publishers.

Unit One provides suggestions for teachers concerning the area of social studies, from a working definition to the organization of the classroom and strategies for planning. Again, as in some of the other sections, it is important for us to look at our students and the school in which we work in deciding how to plan. We also need to look at the experience we have and at our styles of teaching. Although we may plan the best lesson ever taught, the implementation of the lesson and the results, in terms of learning by the students, are what determine its degree of success or failure.

Also, in Unit One, information regarding the use of local resources is discussed. This is an area we often take for granted, but it is hoped that current classroom professionals will take another look at the available resources and that novice educators will begin to develop lists of resources from which they may gain information and be able to provide a more complete social studies program for their students. The educational realm of our country is often the focus of a great deal of negative publicity, but we should remember that the negative publicity often comes because a small number of educators are still focusing on themselves and not the students. In looking at the information provided throughout this project, we should think of why social studies is important as a part of the curriculum and as a part of the ongoing process of preparing our students for the future.

SUGGESTIONS FOR THE FUTURE

As we approach the new century, changes are being made at all levels of the educational realm. Schools are making changes to accommodate the needs of all students by providing more inclusive programs and implementing cultural studies programs. In addition, organization within the schools is changing in order to provide for more input by the classroom professionals and more control through site-based management. As we think about these and other changes that are taking place, we need to prepare ourselves and especially our students to be fully functioning members of the global society in which they will become adults.

Social studies is a diverse area of study, drawing its foundation from a number of other areas. When educators, especially at the elementary and middle school levels, think of social studies instruction, activities to supplement or embellish often come to mind. It is important that we focus on the information to be covered in social studies, and the activities, and present them in a way so as to help students develop an understanding, not just a collection of facts that may or may not be related to activities. For example, teachers must become more cognizant of the skills needed by students and continue to develop methods for helping students implement the use of skills and knowledge in meaningful ways.

As we move into the next century, our students will be a part of an even more diverse society. As we look at the skills they will need to be successful participants, it is important to look at the life experiences of students as well as to the vicarious experiences they have through the media. The vacuum or isolationist view of students in their own little world is not realistic and must not be a part of social studies if we are truly committed to moving our students toward a better understanding of one another and the world in which they live.

Social studies programs that are successful in helping students become productive global citizens will help them to recognize the differences among people (e.g., race, religion, gender) as well as help them focus on the positive effects of having differences. The programs that focus on the positive attributes of all people, while helping students develop the ability to apply skills, including thinking skills, will continue to be valuable in terms of the long-term results.

Instruction in the ability to use thinking skills as a part of social studies will continue to provide students with a method for learning how to work and associate with others. For example, skills such as communication, questioning, drawing conclusions, and making informed decisions are all a part of what social studies instruction should try to help students develop. In addition, skills related to interaction with others are vital to the success of students. These skills, including learning to empathize with others, are a part of what we need to address in social studies.

We, as educators, must continue to be willing to address issues that may be controversial. The issues that relate to real world events, from a historical and contemporary view, which may be presented from an idealized perspective in texts or other materials our students are exposed to, need to be presented factually. If we are to learn from the errors made in the past, we must look realistically at why errors were made and seek not to repeat, or have our students repeat, the same mistakes. In this same vein of thought, it is important to evaluate carefully the students with whom we work in terms of maturity and social experience, as well as the community in which we work, before beginning instruction in areas of controversy. Additionally, we must be aware of our own limitations and biases concerning specific topics. It is inappropriate for educators to expect our students to follow our beliefs. We must distance ourselves from our own beliefs when talking with students about religion or other topics where individual choice should be respected.

In thinking about social studies instruction, it is important to consider the role social studies has in an integrated or umbrella curriculum. Skills and content that are traditionally found in specific areas of the curriculum may be related to social topics. For example, although measuring may be taught in math, it is clearly used in social studies as well. Planning and purposefully showing students how skills may be used in real situations across content areas is of vital importance. Again, however, it must be emphasized that a great deal of time and careful planning must take place so that an appropriate integrated curriculum is developed, rather than a haphazard introduction of disjointed activities. Students must be able to see the relationship of long term learning if this type of curriculum is to be of value.

Finally, students must be at the core of our planning, now and in the future. We must focus on the information they will need in order to be fully productive citizens in a diverse global society. In order to accomplish this daunting task, it is important that we, as educators, continue to learn as much as we can about how individuals learn, what they know at a given time, and based on our best professional knowledge, what we can do in order to help them be successful. We must continue to be aware of our surroundings and address issues related to current affairs as well as help our students develop an understanding of the relationship between past, present, and future.

Appendix

Contents

Preface

The purpose of the appendix is to provide supportive materials to instructors who are using the text. Each unit is divided into four areas:

- an introduction to the material presented in the unit, including advance organizers
- terminology used in that particular unit
- teaching tips with information and ideas to make presentation of the material more functional and interesting
- test questions, which are provided to give some suggestions for possible questions to help the instructor get started in preparing a test

In addition, a section is provided for additional information that may be helpful in preparing handouts to use along with the information covered in the text and manual. These may be copied or modified to meet the individual instructor's needs.

Unit Information

UNIT 1   FOR THE STUDENT/TEACHER

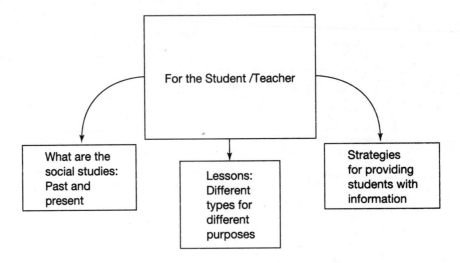

Introduction

In this unit a general discussion concerning the area of social studies is provided. In addition, information that would be helpful to a teacher in planning and implementing instruction is provided.

A number of charts, tables, and inserts provide further explanation that is often needed for students to gain understanding.

Terminology

NCSS	group instruction
expository	simulation
demonstration	expanding environments
mapping	spiraling curriculum
curriculum	directed learning activity
individualized instruction	cooperative learning

Teaching Tips

1. The beginning of this class is a good time for students to reflect on their ideas about social studies. Ask students to list three memories of their own social studies experiences. Share these with the group.

2. If the state education agency has a published curriculum guide, it should be examined in detail to know what expectations are held by the state for the area of social studies instruction. Have a

number of these on hand in class and have students divide into groups to learn more specific information about the guide.

3. Social studies, by definition, is the integration of information from a number of traditional content areas. Have students explore the information they have covered in some of their experiences with the traditional areas and discuss how such information may be important to them as they lead students in learning social studies information.

Test Questions

1. Within the social studies field, a major focus on curriculum development occurred during which decade?
   a. 1930s
   b. 1950s
   c. 1960s
   d. 1980s

2. The most common reason for including current affairs in social studies is to:
   a. introduce students to world events through the media.
   b. require students to learn to read the newspaper.
   c. maintain an up-to-date curriculum.
   d. develop an interest and understanding of world events.

3. As an educator, what do you see as the advantages or disadvantages of an "umbrella" curriculum?

4. Describe a learner involvement lesson. Be sure to include in your discussion a description of the classroom you envision.

UNIT 2   SOCIAL STUDIES TEXTS

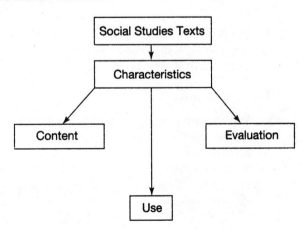

Introduction

One of the major tools often used for instruction in the elementary or middle school classroom is the textbook. In Unit 2, an in-depth discussion of the components of a published program is provided.

Also provided are suggested strategies for evaluation of materials to be used in the classroom. Evaluative instruments are also discussed.

Terminology

scope	tests
sequence	duplicating masters
textbooks	interest inventory
student books	readability
teacher's editions	cloze
workbooks	textbook evaluation
supplemental materials	

Teaching Tips

1. Have students make a comparison of two or three social studies texts. What are the positives and negatives?

2. Students are often asked what they would like to learn about in social studies. Have students complete a poll of ten elementary or middle school students. Are the topics of interest covered in the published program used? Plan how to integrate the topics into the social studies curriculum if they are not covered.

3. If possible, locate a number of older social studies texts. (Check with the local school system or state book depository.) Students should make a comparison of those with the programs currently being used.

4. Interview three or four elementary or middle school teachers. Ask them to explain if and how they use the published social studies program in their classes.

Test Questions

1. Which type of teaching tool is most often used for social studies instruction?
   a. textbooks
   b. computers
   c. films/videos
   d. maps/globes

2. Many teacher's editions of published social studies programs include scope and sequence charts because:
   a. they help educators know the content, concepts, and skills taught at various grade levels.
   b. they provide information about the focus of the materials.
   c. they provide suggestions for instructional strategies.
   d. all of the above.

3. In introducing students to social studies textbooks, teachers should focus attention to:
   a. maps and charts.
   b. table of contents and glossary.
   c. graphs and pictures.
   d. all of the above.

4. Describe how you might use one or two evaluation instruments to decide on the materials best suited for your students.

UNIT 3   MAP AND GLOBE SKILLS

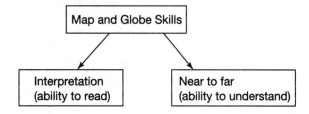

Introduction

While we often take the area of map and globe skills for granted as a part of social studies instruction, it is important for us, as educators, to remember how complex the area really is. In Unit 3 a discussion is provided concerning the need for students not only to be able to interpret or read maps and globes, but to be able to understand the concepts related to reading.

Eight components of map and globe skills are discussed. In addition, for each component, a number of activities are provided.

Terminology

map	symbol
globe	scale
direction	community
location	region

world   graph

nation   contour lines

latitude   senior citizen

longitude

Teaching Tips

1. Have students make a map of another building or grounds where your class is meeting. Students should identify a targeted point. Exchange maps and have students try to locate the targeted point.

2. Salt dough maps are a fun and inexpensive map activity. Teachers need to be aware of the steps involved and the time factor. By making a simple map, these areas as well as other aspects related to map skills may be explored.

   To make a salt dough map:
   a. Identify an area to be mapped (state, country, etc.).
   b. Find a copy of a map of the identified area.
   c. Make an outline on a piece of cardboard (you may have to use an opaque or overhead projector to do this).
   d. Make dough. (See *Recipes.*)
   e. Place dough on map.
   f. Allow map to dry.

3. Correlate art and mapmaking. Have students trace a map on a piece of construction paper. Next, have them glue yarn onto the outline.

Test Questions

1. The study of direction includes the concepts of:
   a. up and down.
   b. the cardinal directions of north, south, east, and west.
   c. the intermediate directions of northeast, southeast, northwest, and southwest.
   d. all of the above.

2. Symbols are used on maps and globes for the following purpose(s):
   a. to represent reality.
   b. to use along with contour lines.
   c. to represent latitude and longitude.
   d. to use instead of coordinates.

3. The study of the community should be limited to:
   a. lower elementary grade levels.
   b. upper elementary grade levels.

       c. middle school levels.
       d. none of the above grade levels.

4. Maps, regions, and location are:
       a. political terms.
       b. economical terms.
       c. geographical terms.
       d. geological terms.

5. Describe an activity you would use with a class to help them learn about the term *nation.* In your description be sure to include the makeup of the class, as well as any other information you would want to consider in using the activity.

UNIT 4 LANGUAGE ARTS AND SOCIAL STUDIES

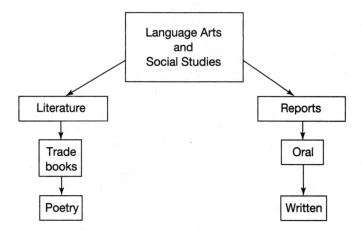

Introduction

What exactly do we mean by language arts? How do we define trade books and how can they be used effectively as a part of social studies instruction? In this section a discussion of the various components of language arts is provided along with suggestions for strategies for including the components of language arts in social studies. In addition, information concerning the use of literature, specifically trade books, is provided.

Terminology

trade books	print-rich environment
fiction	book reports
nonfiction	classroom environment

reference material	presentation
reading	simulations
speaking	prewriting
writing	drafting
listening	revising
KWL	editing
mapping	sharing
oral reports	

Teaching Tips

1. Have students present a trade book. Students should videotape their "book-talk." Have them evaluate their presentation.

2. Invite a librarian to speak to the class about the types of trade books, fiction and nonfiction. If possible, invite a school librarian or a children's librarian.

3. Have students, individually or in small groups, observe a class that has been videotaped. Have students pay particular attention to the effects of the environment on the learning process.

4. Complete a mapping activity with students. (You might look for an interesting topic such as the history of the hamburger.) First have students develop a map based on their knowledge. Then have them read the passage. Finally, they should compare the two maps and see if they can develop a report based on the information.

Test Questions

1. Guidelines for presentations should include all of the following except:
    a. speaking clearly.
    b. the use of graphic aids.
    c. a written copy of the presentation.
    d. a list of possible questions the group may ask.

2. In planning a group presentation, there are four areas that must be addressed. These are:
    a. goal, methods, materials, and presentation.
    b. roles, goal, methods, and presentation.
    c. group size, conflict resolution, aim of report, and materials.
    d. roles, aim of report, materials, and method of presentation.

3. Use of prior knowledge is important in preparing a written report as:

    a. a starting point for locating information.

    b. a means of identifying main concepts to be covered.

    c. a starting point for locating and gathering information.

    d. a means of identifying a topic that is worth investigating.

4. Report topics have been finalized and the students are working through the stages of the writing process. What will you do if one of your students experiences writer's block?

UNIT 5   RELIGION AND SOCIAL STUDIES

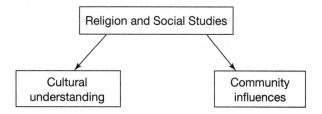

Introduction

We often misunderstand others based on our perception or representations provided by the media. One area that comes into play in understanding the cultural background of others is the influence of religion. While religion is often avoided in the public school area, it is important for educators to look realistically at the relationship between religion and culture.

In Unit 5 the area of religion as a part of cultural understanding in social studies is explored. Also, a number of activities that focus on helping students develop better understanding is provided. The activities provided should be only a part of the information covered in order to help students learn about the influence religion plays in culture.

Terminology

culture	school community
religion	religious groups
global citizens	

Teaching Tips

1. Following a discussion about religion as a cultural influence, have students think about specific religious influences they are familiar with. How might these come into play in the classroom setting?

2. Have students develop lists of trade books that may be useful in helping elementary or middle school students learn about religious and cultural influences. You might also have students bring trade books to class to share.

3. "What Would You Do?" Have students brainstorm about various situations related to religion that might have an effect on their classroom. (You might start off the discussion with information about holiday observances or eating certain foods.)

4. If possible, invite a curriculum coordinator from a local school or school system to discuss the pros and cons of including religion as a part of cultural education. Have students prepare appropriate questions prior to the visit.

Test Questions

1. Community leaders play an important role in religious instruction from a cultural perspective because:
   a. they have a large amount of influence on the local school board.
   b. they may feel threatened.
   c. they may believe it is unnecessary.
   d. all of the above are possible reasons.

2. Religion, as a part of instruction in public schools, is often avoided because:
   a. teachers feel uncomfortable.
   b. instruction in a belief system is against the law.
   c. both a and b.
   d. neither a nor b.

3. Educators need to be knowledgeable of the influence religion plays in culture because:
   a. they are helping prepare students for the future.
   b. some background understanding is needed for instruction.
   c. knowledge helps to prevent perpetuating stereotypes.
   d. all of the above.

4. Describe how you would handle the following situation: A couple of students in your class are not allowed to participate in traditional, school-wide celebrations (e.g., Halloween, Christmas) because of religious beliefs. What could you do to help perpetuate understanding by the rest of the students in your class? How would you make the celebrations more appropriate? (Remember to include age group and makeup of the school community in your description.)

UNIT 6   AMERICAN HERITAGE

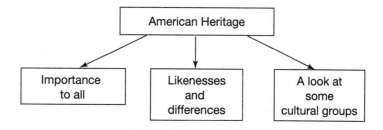

Introduction

Who are we? Where did we come from? Why is it important? In Unit 6 a general discussion is provided concerning a number of the major cultural groups represented in the contemporary citizenry of the United States. Also, suggestions for activities that may serve as a beginning point for instruction are provided.

Terminology

culture	tossed salad
multicultural education	immigrants
native	naturalization
melting pot	refugees

Teaching Tips

1. As a culminating activity, prepare a cultural celebration. The class should be divided into groups and various tasks assigned. The goal is to help students develop a realistic idea of what is required in order to have a celebration. (See additional information in resource section.)

2. If possible, have someone from the U.S. Naturalization Office come to speak to the class. Be sure students have questions prepared for the speaker.

3. Have students identify steps they would take in working with students who have a cultural background different from their own.

4. Have students explore and discuss the various problems that might occur when having a non-English-speaking student in a traditional classroom setting. Students may poll teachers who have been in this situation to find out methods they implemented to be sure learning

was taking place while making the situation as comfortable as possible for all students.

Test Questions

1. To be effective, multicultural education should:
   a. introduce students to the differences among cultures.
   b. change negative attitudes.
   c. be interdisciplinary.
   d. be a combination of all of the above.

2. Today, cultural diversity is seen as:
   a. a weakness.
   b. a point for contempt.
   c. a strength.
   d. both a and b.

3. Focus on the national culture should help students develop:
   a. a sense of belonging.
   b. recognition of the various cultural groups.
   c. social awareness related to our government.
   d. none of the above.

4. Describe the "polka and piñata" approach to multicultural education. Is it appropriate? Why or why not?

UNIT 7   PULLING IT ALL TOGETHER

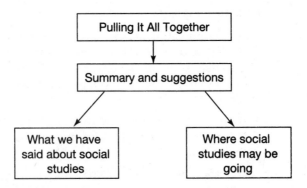

Introduction

In this section, a general discussion or summary of the information covered in the book is readdressed. In addition, a section concerning the needs of students as future global citizens is addressed in terms of what we need to cover as social studies educators. This section differs from the others because its goal is not to serve so much as an instructional tool but as a summary and "think tank" concerning the area of social studies instruction.

Terminology

global citizens   language arts

learner involvement   trade books

religion   published programs

stereotypes   resources

multicultural education   teaching styles

umbrella curriculum   inclusion

map and globe skills   controversial issues

site-based management

Teaching Tips

1. Although a number of areas are addressed in this text, what additional areas are needed in order to better prepare students for life in the next century? Ask students to prepare a list.

2. Have students investigate recent research related to inclusion as a means for grouping students for instruction. Be sure to define the term for students as well as provide additional information such as videos or appropriate handouts. Discuss the differences among traditional grouping methods and those encouraged as a part of inclusion.

3. The term "umbrella curriculum" has been used in reference to the area of social studies instruction. Have students investigate and discuss this term. Be sure to include information gathered from local educators regarding the term.

4. We often think of empowerment for students in terms of their ability to work independently and think for themselves. What terms are currently being used in relation to school-based professionals being empowered? How does this differ from traditional management plans? What are the ramifications of this for educators as related to the area of social studies?

Test Questions

1. Controversial issues are best handled by teaching from a factual perspective. Identify one controversial issue and provide an

explanation of how you might address the issue during instruction. Remember: The school, community, age of students, maturity of students, and your background all play a part in how you would address an issue. Include any pertinent information.

2. Learner involvement is a key term mentioned throughout the text. Define the term and explain why it is important in social studies instruction.

3. Published programs have made great strides in a number of areas. Describe how you might effectively use the published program as a part of social studies instruction.

4. Describe an activity you would use with a class in which social studies would serve as an umbrella curriculum. In your description be sure to include the makeup of the class, as well as any other information you would want to consider in using the activity.

Additional Information

GUIDELINES FOR OBSERVATION

As a part of your social studies methods course, you are required to observe or teach lessons at a local elementary or middle school. There are a number of guidelines that you should follow regarding the visits. While some of these are only "common sense," there may be other areas that you have not thought of.

Please read and follow each of the following suggestions.

1. Upon receiving your placement notification, call to find out about or to set up a time for an initial visit. During this call, find out if there is a special place where you should park.

2. Dress appropriately! (No jeans or shorts!) Be conservative! Men should wear dress slacks, shirt, tie, socks, and regular shoes (not sports shoes); women should wear a dress or skirt (of knee length and not tight) and blouse and flats or low pumps.

    You may ask your cooperating teacher about appropriate attire for the following visits. Even within a school system, dress codes (unwritten) vary from school to school.

3. Arrive a few minutes early for your scheduled initial appointment and also for all following visits.

    If you are not familiar with the location of the school, you might consider making a trial run prior to the initial visit. Remember, the time of day when you will be at the school will need to be considered in terms of traffic, etc.

4. For the initial visit, you may be meeting with the principal, assistant principal, and the cooperating teacher. You will want to find out where the classroom in which you will be working is located. In addition, you may receive a booklet about the school or a tour of the school.

    If an information sheet has not been provided to your cooperating teacher by the clinical experience office, you may want to provide a one or two page information sheet in your first meeting with the cooperating teacher. Include such information as your name, major, past experiences with students and children, your interests as related to teaching, and any other information you feel would be helpful.

    Also, be sure to offer to share your home phone number with the cooperating teacher. In the event that you need to reschedule an observation or lesson, this would be most helpful (e.g., you probably wouldn't want to observe a substitute).

5. For all visits, be sure to check in at the main office. Most schools require that all persons visiting in a school wear a badge, as well as identify where or with whom they may be working. This helps them to know who is in the school as well as know where to find you if you are needed.

6. While observing, make mental notes. Write as little as possible while in the classroom, unless otherwise requested to do so. After you leave, you may rewrite or type your notes. You may want to set aside a time to review your notes with your cooperating teacher if requested to do so.

7. Be sure to get all signatures needed on verification forms or any other forms that may be required (e.g., feedback forms, rating forms).

8. Always be sure to check out through the main office and return any badges.

9. Following your final visit, be sure to send your cooperating teacher and the class a thank-you note.

10. You might also want to send the principal and/or assistant principal a thank-you note following your final visit.

Social Studies: Observation #1

Student: _____ Student #: _____

Date: _____ Time of Day: _____

Teacher Observed: _____ School: _____

Grade Observed: _____

General makeup of the class (number of students, boys, girls, cultural diversity within class, ability levels in class):

Physical attributes of the classroom (a sketch of the room, number of bulletin boards, windows, placement of student and teacher desks):

Daily class schedule (note the time especially devoted to social studies):

Management/discipline plan followed in class (classroom rules):

Date due: _____

Social Studies: Observation #2

Student: _____ Student #: _____

Date: _____ Time of Day: _____

Teacher Observed: _____ School: _____

Grade Observed: _____

Specific Purpose(s)/Goal(s) of Lesson Observed: _____

_____

_____

Areas of observation: *My reaction:*

Materials used:

_____

Methods and procedures:

_____

Pupil response and participation:

_____

Pupil–teacher relationships:

_____

General atmosphere of class:

_____

Assignments:

Date due: _____

Social Studies: Observation #3

Student: _____ Student #: _____

Date: _____ Time of Day: _____

Teacher Observed: _____ School: _____

Grade Observed: _____

Specific Purpose(s)/Goal(s) of Lesson Observed: _____

_____

_____

Areas of observation: *My reaction:*

Materials used by the teacher:

   audiovisual materials?
   books other than texts?
   encyclopedias/reference materials?

Materials used by the students:

   audiovisual materials?
   books other than texts?
   encyclopedias/reference materials?

Methods and procedures:

   whole group?
   small group?
   cooperative learning groups?
   peer tutoring?
   learning/interest centers?

Pupil response and participation:

   rules for interaction?
   levels of questions used?
   active learner involvement?
   lecture?

General atmosphere of class (Summarize your visit. Include any important or unique information.):

Date due: _____

QUESTIONING

One area of weakness for a number of educators, novice and experienced, is the area of questioning. While we are familiar with such information as the importance of questioning from courses in educational psychology and classroom management, sometimes bridging that information into the content arena is not considered. It is important that we encourage our students to think critically and creatively throughout the curriculum.

In social studies, we focus a great deal on interaction and discussion. While published programs usually provide leading questions for discussion, it is important that the classroom professional evaluate the material and topic being covered in formulating questions for his or her own classroom situation.

Questions should be planned in advance and be sequenced so as to lead from text-based questions to those that encourage creative or critical thinking.

Questions for the Classroom

Recognition and Recall

1. Facts

   Who did ———————?

   When did ———————?

   How many———————?

   What are ———————?

2. Definitions

   What is meant by ———————?

   What does ——————— mean?

   What meaning did you understand for ———————?

   Define ———————.

   Explain what we mean by ———————.

3. Generalizations

   What events led to ———————?

How did _____ and _____ cause _____?

What is the relationship between _____ and _____?

4. Value judgement

What is said about _____?

Do you agree?

What kind of girl was _____?

What did _____ do that you wouldn't?

Expressing Ideas in a Different Way

Write a story pretending you are _____.

What does the author mean by _____?

What kind of drawing could you make to illustrate _____?

Tell me in your own words _____?

Understanding Relationships

1. Are the ideas the same, different, related, or opposite?

How is _____ like _____?

Is _____ the same as _____? Why or why not?

Compare _____ with _____.

How does _____ today resemble _____ in _____?

2. Development of an idea based on information in the passage

What will _____ and _____ lead to?

If _____ continues to _____, what might happen?

What would happen if _____?

3. Inductive thinking

What facts in the passage support the idea that _____?

What events led to _____? Why?

4. Quantitative thinking

    How much has ————————— increased?

    How many causes of ————————— can you list?

    What conclusions can you draw from the graph/figure on page ——?

5. Cause and effect

    Why did ————————— happen?

    How did ————————— make ————————— happen?

    What two things led up to —————————?

Application—Using a Combination of Types of Thinking to Solve a Problem

How can we show that we need a safety patrol at the south end of the school?

If we were on a deserted island, what would we need to do first?

How can we build a playground in the vacant lot next to the school?

Analysis—Using Logic to Solve a Problem

One settlement was attacked by a certain tribe of Native Americans. Then settlers disliked all Native Americans. Were they right or wrong in their feelings? Why?

Synthesis—Using Creative Thinking to Solve a Problem

What other titles could be used for the story about —————————?

What other ending could have taken place if —————————?

If ————————— had not —————————, what might have happened?

Evaluation—Making Judgements Based on Defined Standard

Did you enjoy the passage about —————————? Why or why not?

In the text, the information says that the ————————— felt —————————. Is this a fact or opinion?

Write a short story about your favorite person in history. Why is this person your favorite?

RESOURCES RELATED TO SOCIAL STUDIES

American Anthropological Association
1703 New Hampshire Ave. NW
Washington, DC 20009

Foundation for Teaching Economics
550 Kearney St., Ste 1000
San Francisco, CA 94108

Joint Council on Economic Education
2 Park Ave.
New York, NY 10016

National Council for Geographic
Education
Western Illinois University
Macomb, IL 61455

American Historical Association
400 A St. SE
Washington, DC 20003

Society for History Education
California State University
170 E Seventh St.
Long Beach, CA 90840

American Psychological Association
1200 Seventeenth St. NW
Washington, DC 20036

American Economic Association
1313 Twenty-first Ave. S
Nashville, TN 37212

Association for American
Geographers
1710 Sixteenth St. SW
Washington, DC 20009

American Geographical Society
Broadway at 156th St.
New York, NY 10032

Organization of American Historians
112 N. Bryan St.
Bloomington, IN 47401

American Political Science
Association
1517 New Hampshire Ave. NW
Washington, DC 20036

American Sociological Association
1722 N St. NW
Washington, DC 20036

GENERAL RESOURCES

National Wildlife Federation
1413 Sixteenth St. NW
Washington, DC 20036

Antidefamation League of B'nai B'rith
823 United Nations Plaza
New York, NY 10017

Constitution Rights Foundation
601 South Kingsley Dr.
Los Angeles, CA 90005

United Nations Sales Section
Room 2300
United Nations Headquarters
New York, NY 10017

World Future Studies
4916 St. Elmo
Bethesda, MD 20814

National Association of Ethnic Studies
1861 Rosemont
Claremont, CA 91711

Population Reference Bureau
1755 Massachusetts Ave. NW
Washington, DC 20036

Superintendent of Documents
United States Government Printing
Office
Washington, DC 20402

REPORTING INFORMATION TO CAREGIVERS

The adults in a student's life are vital members of the team involved in the learning process. In order for them to be successful in their roles, it is important that they be constantly aware of the information being covered in the social studies classroom as well as how well the student is progressing. While personal contact through conferences is vital, and general reporting of academic achievement is reported via some formal system in almost all education realms, additional written communication should be considered important.

In order to encourage involvement, outlines of information that is to be studied could be sent home. The outline should give target areas of study, activities that may be ongoing as a part of the study, and information such as page numbers to be read in the text or trade books that might be read to supplement the study. (See Figure 1.)

Another suggestion that may be implemented to keep caregivers and students informed is that of a progress report. Some reports are given in terms of academic grades, others are checklists of skills or topics with a "+" or "−" to indicate mastery. Information on some reports are limited to content while others include information about participation, behavior, or general citizenship. In addition, there are reports that are simply brief notes about the student's success. There are also reports which are a combination of several of those mentioned. (See Figures 2 and 3.)

While there are a number of formats available, it is important that the teacher decides on the form that is best suited for his or her purposes. In order to help you think about the type of form you might use, think about questions such as these:

1. What types of comments should be included?
2. Would you want to establish different reporting methods for students in elementary or middle school levels? Primary or intermediate levels?
3. What information is most likely to be helpful to parents? Students?

LEARNING ABOUT US: A CULTURAL CELEBRATION

Cultural Celebration: Suggested Guidelines

Rationale for a Cultural Celebration

1. Engages students in an in-depth study of a topic.
2. Provides opportunities for a look at the differences and likenesses of cultures.

FIGURE 1

SEPTEMBER

SUNDAY	MONDAY	TUESDAY	WEDNESDAY	THURSDAY	FRIDAY	SATURDAY
		1 First day of School Welcome Back!	2 Getting to Know You – Interest Inventory	3 Neighborhood Text pages 1-10	4 Review info. in text	5
6	7 Labor Day Holiday	8 Language Exp. Activity Bring 3 bits of infor. to school to share	9 Community Text pages 11-15 (A skit will be presented on 18th at 1:30-Please Come!)	10 Discussion also follow up puzzle	11 WEAR Comfortable shoes – a walk around the school neighborhood!	12
13	14 Text pages 16-20 Activity related to text and walk on last Fri.	15 Puppet skit role assignments "These Are the People in Our Neighborhood"	16 Practice Skit : Talk about the roles and why each is important	17 Practice Skit: Work behind puppet stage	18 SKIT Presentation 1:30	19
20	21 Class big book development: Our Own Community	22 Mapping our Community	23 Continue Mapping Activity	24 From my house to school: Bring in info. to help you with your map!	25 Finished maps Discuss and display!	26
27	28 Community workers Why each is important!	29 Visit Grocery Store $3.00 needed for each student purchase.	30 Visitor: Veterinarian and Friends	1 Visitor: Pizza Maker and Friends (We will have pizza for snack. Join us.)	2 What we have learned	

FIGURE 2

Grades For _____ Six Weeks

Student: _Julie Parent_   Dates: _9/5_ - _9/22_

Subject	Week 1	Week 2	Week 3	Week 4	Week 5	Week 6
MATH	30/30 A	20/20 A	24/30 B 20/20 A			
SCIENCE-HEALTH	12/15 B	☺	8/10 B			
SOCIAL STUDIES	90/100 A	10/10 A	6/8 B 7/7 A			
ENGLISH	17/20 B	15/15 A	25/27 A 15/15 A			
WRITING	☺	20/20 A	20/20 A			
READING	☺	10/10 A	9/10 A 10/20 C See sheet!			
SPELLING	15/15 A	19/20 A	19/20 A NB✓ WB✓			
CITIZEN-SHIP	A+ ☺	A+ ☺	A+ ☺			

Parent's Signature	Comments
1. _Ima Parent_	
2. _Ima Parent_	Julie really has enjoyed having you for her 3rd grade teacher.
3. _Ima Parent_	
4.	
5.	
6.	

FIGURE 3

Grades For _____ Six Weeks

Student: _____ Dates: _____ - _____

Subject	Week 1	Week 2	Week 3	Week 4	Week 5	Week 6
MATH						
SCIENCE-HEALTH						
SOCIAL STUDIES						
ENGLISH						
WRITING						
READING						
SPELLING						
CITIZEN-SHIP						

Parent's Signature	Comments
1.	
2.	
3.	
4.	
5.	
6.	

3. Provides an ongoing part of multicultural education.
4. Provides for integration of a number of traditional content areas.

Participant Responsibilities

1. Research the culture and country of origin in depth (e.g., history, government, people).
2. Provide a map of the country that shows its location in relation to other countries.
3. Prepare a display of artifacts of the culture or country of origin (e.g., foods, music, traditional celebration information).
4. Develop a booklet identifying key concepts and important information about the culture and country of origin.

RECIPES AND OTHER SUGGESTIONS

Salt Dough Recipe

Materials

    1 cup salt   1 cup plain flour

    water

Directions

Mix equal parts of salt and flour with enough water to ensure a plastic consistency. The mixture can be placed on a map that is outlined on cardboard. Terrain can be molded to make it more realistic. Food coloring or tempera paint may be added. Watercolors may be used to paint in rivers.

Play Dough (Modeling) Recipe

Materials

    3 cups plain flour   1 cup salt

    water

Directions

Mix together three cups flour and one cup salt. Stir and knead these materials together. Add water gradually until the mixture has the consistency of dough. Dry tempera paint may be added to make it more colorful.

Liberian Rice Bread

Materials

2 cups cream of rice	1½ cups mashed ripe bananas
3 tablespoons sugar	2 eggs
4 teaspoons baking powder	1½ cups milk
½ teaspoon salt	1 cup oil

Directions

Grease 8″ × 12″ pan, preheat oven to 375 degrees. Mix dry ingredients. Gradually add bananas, milk, and eggs. Add oil and then blend thoroughly. Pour into pan and bake for 45 minutes.

Cornhusk Dolls

Materials

corn husks	markers
string	

Directions

Using corn husks, make the head, body, and arms. Tie them on to the body with the string. Students add facial features and clothing decorations using markers.

Fry Bread

Materials

3 cups self-rising flour	1 cup warm water
1½ teaspoons baking powder	large bottle cooking oil

Directions

Sift the flour and baking powder together. Make a hole in the center of flour and pour in water. Stir until it forms a smooth ball. Knead on a floured board for about 3 minutes. Allow it to rise for about 30 minutes and knead again. Cut off small pieces and stretch out flat (like a thin pancake). Cut a slit in the center and drop it into hot cooking oil. Fry until golden brown. Serve with jelly, jam, or syrup.

Making Jewelry

Materials

²/₃ cup salt	food coloring
¹/₂ cup flour	needle or toothpick
¹/₃ cup water	thread
paper plates	waxed paper

Directions

Mix the salt, flour, and water together. Cook over a hot stove until thick. Allow to cool on a plate and knead until pliable. Give each student some dough and have them mold it into small balls or shapes for jewelry. Puncture a hole through each bead or shape before it dries, using a toothpick or needle. Dry the beads on waxed paper. Finally, thread the beads on thread to make necklaces.

Papier-mâché Masks

Materials

newspaper or paper towels	balloons
liquid starch	paint

Directions

Cut newspaper or paper towels into strips about ¹/₂- to ³/₄-inch wide. Dip into a bowl of liquid starch. Run through fingers, squeezing off excess. Arrange strips on an inflated balloon. Allow to dry on a newspaper-covered flat surface for two or three days. After thoroughly dry, the mask can be painted or decorated as desired. Surface features may be added by adding layers.

Soap Carving

Materials

soap bars	plastic knives

Directions

Students should be given a bar of soft soap (such as Ivory) and a plastic knife. After deciding on a figure to be carved, students should begin to shape their figures. Simple figures should be encouraged such as a fish or a bear.

Sock Puppets

Materials

socks	glue gun (optional)
needle and thread	decorative material (e.g., buttons, yarn)

Directions

Take an old sock. Sew on buttons, yarn, or other materials to fit the situation. Older students will enjoy making their own. If adult supervision is supplied, a hot glue gun may be used.

Stick Puppets

Materials

poster board or drawing paper	markers
old magazines (optional)	craft sticks
glue	

Directions

On a piece of poster board or drawing paper, draw a head and leave a tab at the bottom. (Pictures may also be cut from magazines.) Glue these onto tongue depressors or craft sticks.

Paper Bag Puppets

Materials

paper bags	markers
newspaper or tissue	string

Directions

Draw a face on the bag, stuff it partially with newspaper or tissue. Tie at the bottom (leaving enough room to use as a grip). Add appropriate decorations.

Index

NOTES